Literacy Remix

Bridging Adolescents' In and Out of School Literacies

Jesse Gainer   **Diane Lapp**

INTERNATIONAL
Reading Association
800 BARKSDALE ROAD, PO BOX 8139
NEWARK, DE 19714-8139, USA
www.reading.org

The International Reading Association attempts, through its publications, to provide a forum for a wide spectrum of opinions on reading. This policy permits divergent viewpoints without implying the endorsement of the Association.

Executive Editor, Books   Corinne M. Mooney
Developmental Editor   Charlene M. Nichols
Developmental Editor   Tori Mello Bachman
Developmental Editor   Stacey L. Reid
Editorial Production Manager   Shannon T. Fortner
Design and Composition Manager   Anette Schuetz

Project Editors   Tori Mello Bachman and Susanne Viscarra

Cover   Design, Brad Tillinghast; DJ graphic, Benjamin Wachenje / Digital Vision (RF) / Jupiterimages; book graphic, Shutterstock

The publisher would appreciate notification where errors occur so that they may be corrected in subsequent printings and/or editions.

Library of Congress Cataloging-in-Publication Data
Gainer, Jesse, 1967–
   Literacy remix : bridging adolescents in and out of school literacies / by Jesse Gainer and Diane Lapp.
      p. cm.
   Includes bibliographical references and index.
   ISBN 978-0-87207-800-0 (alk. paper)
   1. Language arts (Middle school) 2. Language arts (Secondary) 3. Blended learning.
I. Lapp, Diane. II. Title.
   LB1631.G154 2010
   428.0071'2—dc22

                                                                                          2009049964

CONTENTS

Jesse Gainer is an assistant professor of education in the Department of Curriculum and Instruction at Texas State University, San Marcos, Texas, USA. He teaches undergraduate and graduate classes in both university- and field-based settings. He has taught bilingual elementary and Reading Recovery, and has worked in middle and high school settings.

His major areas of research and instruction include critical media literacy and issues of language, literacy, and culture. He can be reached at jg51@txstate.edu.

Diane Lapp is a distinguished professor in the School of Teacher Education at San Diego State University (SDSU), San Diego, California, USA. She has taught in elementary and middle school, and is currently an 11th- and 12th-grade English teacher. Her major areas of research and instruction center on issues related to struggling readers and writers who live in economically deprived settings and their families.

She directs and teaches field-based preservice and graduate programs and courses and served as the coeditor of California's literacy journal, *The California Reader,* from 1999 to 2007. She has also authored, coauthored, and edited many articles, columns, texts, handbooks, and children's materials on reading and language arts issues.

Diane has also chaired and cochaired several committees for the International Reading Association (IRA) and the National Reading Conference. Her many educational awards include being named as the Outstanding Teacher Educator and Faculty Member in the School of Teacher Education at SDSU, the Distinguished Research Lecturer from SDSU's Graduate Division of Research, and IRA's 1996 Outstanding Teacher Educator of the Year. Diane is also a member of the California Reading Association Hall of Fame and the Reading Hall of Fame. She can be reached at lapp@mail.sdsu.edu.

CHAPTER 1

Promoting Literacy Learning Through a Remix of Our Old and New Understandings About Literacy Instruction

If literacy educators continue to define literacy in terms of alphabetic practice only, in ways that ignore, exclude or devalue new-media texts, they not only abdicate a professional responsibility to describe the ways in which humans are now communicating and making meaning, but they also run the risk of the curriculum no longer holding relevance for students who are communicating in increasingly expansive networked environments.

Selfe & Hawisher, 2004

Considering the above quote, each of us needs to ask, How well are we communicating via new literacies? Wikis, blogs, search engines, instant messaging, tweeting, texting, sampling, bubbling, online gaming, mashups, fan fiction, Web 2.0, new literacies, anime, manga, YouTube—these are some of the terms you probably hear from your students with continuing frequency. These terms have become Tier 1 words for many students in today's classrooms, because these words are the basic vocabulary occurring in students' daily spoken language (Beck, McKeown, & Kucan, 2002). Some may seem to be Tier 2 words that are used by those you deem as sophisticated speakers who sound like a technology book you haven't read. Or you may even label these as more difficult Tier 3 words that you only hear in isolated situations.

These words are labels for new technologies that "require new literacies to effectively exploit their potentials" (Leu, Kinzer, Coiro, & Cammack, 2004, p. 1572). Adding new literacies has become quite common as we send a message via an information communication technology (ICT) such as text messaging (or texting), Twitter, Facebook, or e-mail, search for information via the Internet, and read a wide array of texts on our Kindles. It seems that just as we've gained some proficiency with one of these new literacies, we hear of others that offer us additional ways to gain information and share communications. As noted by Leu et al. (2004),

> The new literacies of the Internet and other ICTs include the skills, strategies, and dispositions necessary to successfully use and adapt to the rapidly changing information and communication technologies and contexts that continuously emerge in our world and influence all areas of our personal and professional lives. These new literacies allow us to use the Internet and other ICTs to identify important questions, locate information, critically evaluate the usefulness of that information, synthesize information to answer those questions, and then communicate the answers to others. (p. 1572)

As educators, we know the enthusiasm we personally have for learning how to effectively use these expanded Internet and ICT literacies, and we certainly see their use by our students. Using and observing the use of new literacies has expanded our definition of what constitutes literacy and caused many of us to explore how they can positively impact classroom practice. These new literacies certainly offer additional opportunities to engage and teach our students. In reality, inclusion of new literacies needs to become part of our instructional base if we want to engage students in motivating, purposeful learning experiences that move us from being teachers who "assume all of the responsibility for performing a task...to a situation in which students assume all of the responsibility" (Duke & Pearson, 2002, p. 211).

Are you wondering how to accommodate these ever-expanding new literacies in your daily instruction? If so, you are like many others— including both of us. Before we go any further, a caveat is in order. We, the authors, are not experts in technology, nor do we expect this from the majority of teachers. In fact in some ways, our lack of technical expertise serves us in our quest to share power relationships with students. We teachers bring certain strengths to the table in terms of our teaching; however, we also recognize that students enter our classrooms with a wealth of knowledge and a lot to offer, and we hope to tap this for instruction. Our use of technology is but a tool to facilitate the building of bridges between the literacies of our students' out-of-school lives, our classrooms, and the greater world in which we live. This is how we envision remixing new literacies and what is currently known about effective literacy instruction and learning. We'll explore the traditional definition of *remix* a bit further in Chapter 2.

Owning the Idea of Remixing New Literacies and Existing Instruction

To get started, complete the chart in Table 1, which is a personal assessment of your understanding of new literacies. We'd like you to continually return to this chart to reflect on the new literacies vocabulary and instructional insights you're acquiring as you share the ideas we've presented throughout this text.

Did you feel somewhat overwhelmed by this task? That's how students often feel when they are presented with a list of words they don't own. We believe that *owning* a word means that it is a part of one of our Discourses (Gee, 1996) and that its use can be extended to new Discourse communities we join. Gee (1996) explains how our various Discourses help us navigate different social spaces:

> Discourses are ways of being in the world, or forms of life which integrate words, acts, values, beliefs, attitudes, and social identities, as well as gestures, glances, body positions, and clothes. A Discourse is a sort of identity kit, which comes complete with the appropriate costume and instructions on how to act, talk, and often write, so as to take on a particular social role that others recognize. (p. 127)

Think about all of your Discourse communities. Which of these is foregrounded at any given time, dependent on the situation and the people with whom you are interacting? As you move from one situation to the next, you draw on the Discourse you have for a successful interaction. Have you ever found yourself in an important situation that required a Discourse that you hadn't fully developed? Did you feel anxious and not smart? This is where many educators find themselves daily as they overhear their students engaged in new literacies Discourse. This is a common feeling among many teachers as we hear our students talk about MySpace, blogs, and chatting with friends on iChat or Skype. Many of us are the immigrants to this discourse, whereas our students under the age of 25 are the natives. They grew up never knowing a time when there were no cell phones, and the Internet has always been part of their lives (Prensky, 2001, 2005). With this realization let's think about our students and how we can utilize their interests in and knowledge of all of these new literacies to support their continued learning. This will involve a remixing of all the knowledge we have about our students, effective literacy, and new literacies instruction.

Table 1. Personal Assessment of New Literacies Language

Term	I Know It and Can Define It	Go Ahead and Define It	I've Integrated This Into My Instruction	I've Heard of It, but I'm Not Sure What It Means	I've Never Heard of It
Anime					
Blog					
Bubbling					
Facebook™					
Fan fiction					
Flickr™					
Google™					
Hip-hop					
Instant messaging					
iPhone®					
Manga					
Mashup					
Meme					
Online gaming					
Podcast					
Remixing					
Sampling					
Search engine					
Skype™					
Texting/text messaging					
Tweeting					
Twitter™					
Viral video					
Web 2.0					
Wiki					
Wikipedia™					
YouTube™					

Reading Habits of an Adolescent Reader

Let's think about the literacy habits of adolescents. The first word that should pop into our minds is that there are *differences* in what adolescents like to read, how they like to read, how well they can read, and how they like to share their responses and insights. Just like all other groups of readers, there is also a range among adolescents from those who can but don't read outside of school to those who read every chance they get. This range continues to be evidenced by data from the National Assessment of Educational Progress, which notes that three quarters of adolescent readers in grade 8 have consistently scored above a basic level of competency for the last 15 years (Lee, Grigg, & Donahue, 2007). What about the others? What about moving all of these students to proficient or advanced levels of literacy? What will it take? We believe supporting literacy learning gains for all students takes well planned, explicit, motivating instruction that builds on each student's knowledge base and learning behaviors. Because we believe that this is possible, we share examples of teachers who have added a motivating new literacies dimension to their instruction. We call this a remixing of all of their expertise.

Are Students Reading?

In the 12th-grade class that Diane (author) teaches, she has one student who lays her head on her desk every chance she gets so that she can read from the two or three extra books, on a range of topics, that she carries in her backpack. This is in addition to the book club and independent reading selections that are being read by her and all of her classmates. In this same classroom, there are students who read only what is assigned and a few others who, for myriad reasons, come to school not having read text segments that their group agreed to read. This range of readers and what they read is representative of other adolescents' in-school reading habits.

Although these students might not read all the time, they are very literate people. Many have pages on Facebook and MySpace. Most send and read instant messages on iChat and text message each other on their cell phones throughout the day. The majority also blog and move easily among multiple online sources that connect them to information containing visuals, print, and sound. Many also produce, consume, and share teen zines and graphic novels (Alvermann & Heron, 2001). Is it any wonder then that some of them do not enjoy reading linearly in a traditional text format when they have expanded access to information digitally through hypermediated texts? This is why we, as educators, must remix the best of existing instruction and new literacies.

Ownership Supports Engagement

As you observe adolescents, it becomes obvious that much is going on in their outside-of-school literacy lives, which is why it's so important to invite them to draw from their exciting sociocultural experiences. Students also need to have a voice in how these can be integrated into the learning culture of the classroom. One factor that does seem to drive all students' reading is that they are much more interested and engaged when they are involved in selecting the text as well as the medium for accessing it. Their participation also seems to be piqued when they are invited to share their thinking through self-selected digital displays rather than handwritten contexts. It is then that their ethos connects with their technological knowledge (Lankshear & Knobel, 2002; Lapp & Fisher, 2009). This sense of ownership in their learning increases students' levels of engagement and motivation (Sutherland, Botzakis, Moje, & Alvermann, 2008). If you are teaching adolescents and considering planning instruction that draws from their interests and practices, it's important to talk with your students about these literacy practices and observe who is motivated by each type of new literacy. This insight can help you plan curricular projects that draw on students' self-selected and learned technological resources. Your attempts to validate students' out-of-school literacy practices and then utilize and integrate them into in-school learning tasks that support content area learning are well founded.

Many educators agree that what constitutes instruction for adolescent learners must be more attentive to their interests and strengths and less focused on the whole-class reading of novels and content-specific textbooks, which do not seem to be working for many adolescents (Alvermann, Moon, & Hagood, 1999; Fisher & Ivey, 2007; Moore, Bean, Birdyshaw, & Rycik, 1999). Engaged learning can occur if their outside-of-school knowledge and interests are acknowledged, respected, and used as part of the instructional picture within the culture of the classroom. As a result, within-class experiences become the bases for what continues to be learned after the school day ends and well into life. This seamless connection says to students that their interests are important and are what should motivate their desire to learn long after they leave school.

Expanding Your New Literacies Discourse

To help you move from having a basic understanding of new literacies terms to easily integrating them into your instructional plan, we'll use them in context as we share instructional examples throughout this book. Also, Table 2 lists simple definitions for new literacies terms for quick reference.

Table 2. New Literacies Terms Defined

Term	Definition
Anime	Japanese animation contained in many graphic novels
Blog	An online journal, which can be written by individuals or groups, that contains entries in reverse chronological order with the most recent at the top and often contains images and links to other websites as well as topical commentary
Bubbling	Inserting a speech bubble, usually in a cartoon or graphic, to add commentary; often used as a form of social critique in critical media literacy
Facebook™	A hugely popular, online social networking website that connects people worldwide
Fan fiction	A new book, story, or series that allows fans to add a character or episode
Flickr™	A host site that allows users to upload and share images and videos
Google™	An online search engine (Due to its popularity, "to google" is now also a commonly used verb form meaning to search online using www.google.com.)
Hip-hop	A cultural, artistic movement rooted in the experiences of disenfranchised urban youth and often manifested in break dancing, graffiti, deejaying, and rap
Instant messaging	An online, interactive message tool that allows you to create a list of "buddies" with whom you can communicate continuously and simultaneously when they are also online
iPhone®	A mobile phone that offers many online features and applications (or apps) in addition to chatting and texting, including information storage and access
Manga	A Japanese comic book in which the art style is much more exaggerated than the classic U.S. comic book. Almost always written in black and white, unlike multicolor U.S. comic books, manga also is usually smaller in trim size but is similar to a novel in page count. The pace of the story moves more quickly in manga, which is usually created by one person, unlike a U.S. comic book, which is typically produced by several people.
Mashup	An overlay of the vocal tracks of one or more songs over the music track of another or a blending of video and other text sources
Meme	A concept, catchphrase, or inside joke that spreads quickly via the Internet
Online gaming	Online games that are played independently or within an online community in virtual worlds on some form of computer network and contain a range of graphics and virtual worlds

(continued)

Table 2. New Literacies Terms Defined (*continued*)

Term	Definition
Podcast	An online audio or video recording that can be accessed in real-time or downloaded to experience at a later time (A vodcast is a video-only podcast.)
Remixing	Combining and manipulating cultural artifacts such as songs to create new media
Sampling	A technique that involves taking a portion (or sample) of a song and reusing it in a new song
Search engine	An online tool, such as Firefox™, Safari®, and Bing™, for searching information on the Web
Skype™	A downloadable software program that allows users to see and speak to each other via the Internet by using this software with a webcam and microphone
Texting/ text messaging	Exchanging brief, typed messages between mobile phones
Twitter™	A free social networking and microblogging service that provides users with the ability to send and read personal messages (or "tweets")
Viral video	A video clip that spreads quickly via the Internet
Web 2.0	Refers to the ways people can interact and construct knowledge collectively, largely as a result of technological developments, such as social networking sites, wikis, and other interactive technologies that allow users to control data
Wiki	A website whose content can be collaboratively edited by anyone who has Internet access, such as www.wikipedia.com
Wikipedia™	A free, online encyclopedia wiki that offers instant information on most topics and not only allows users to read text but also to edit, revise, and add information
YouTube™	A video-sharing website that allows users to upload and share personal videos and also view and comment on videos shared by others

Through these examples, we hope you'll see how we and other teachers engage and teach students by modeling new information and strategies, providing differentiated feedback, encouraging and supporting peers within a variety of group configurations, and allowing ample time for students to move from practice to ownership of the new information.

These examples are situated within a gradual release of learning model, which illustrates intentional instructional planning, delivery, and assessment of student performance and shifts responsibility for extending the newly learned knowledge to the learner to use independently (Fisher & Frey, 2008; Pearson & Gallagher, 1983; Vygotsky, 1978). A gradual release of learning occurs as the teacher first models how to do a specified task and then supports the students as they gain the knowledge and skills needed to perform independently. This gradual release is similar to when you first learned to ride a bike, read a book, or use word-processing software: An expert modeled for you and then supported you until you reached a level of independent proficiency.

What Constitutes Powerful Instruction?

As we consider the changing landscape of 21st-century literacies and the changing demands that ensue for citizens of this century, we must look to ways that schools can prepare young people to be successful. Although schools are often slow to respond to change, and many schools lack sufficient resources to stay at the cusp of technological developments, teachers must continue to adapt our instruction to meet the needs of our increasingly diverse and technologically savvy student population.

How to provide the best possible learning experiences for every student is a question that vexes every teacher at every grade level, especially since the gap between students who struggle with learning and their peers continues to accelerate (Torgesen et al., 2007). Like many educators, we believe it is possible to close this gap if teachers implement sound research-based motivational instruction. So we have designed examples of research-based motivational literacy instruction for adolescent learners that remix new literacies and what is currently known about effective instruction, and we present these throughout this book. Each of these examples can be replicated and expanded by using Table 3 to support your planning. We often refer to this chart while sharing the instructional examples.

There is no mystery about what constitutes effective research-based literacy instruction. In their report to the Carnegie Corporation of New York, Biancarosa and Snow (2004) and a team of educators identify instructional and administrative elements from existing research that are known to support literacy growth for adolescent learners. As you can see from the following list, these elements focus on the teacher, the student, and the context of instruction. The *teacher* plans and shares

- Focused, explicit instruction embedded in language arts and content area content

Table 3. Remixing: Focused Instruction and New Literacies Learning

Teacher's Considerations	Guiding Questions
Direct, explicit instruction	• What are the instructional goals? • What standards are being addressed?
Diverse texts	• What is the range of the reading/literacy proficiencies among your students? • What topics interest your students?
Technology component	• What technologies are familiar to you? • What technologies are motivating to your students?
Collaborative learning	• What tasks can students perform based on their knowledge and literacies? • How do these various tasks support completion of the goals, problems, or project?
Intensive writing	• Are the writing tasks integrated throughout the content tasks? • Are the writing tasks varied to support students' strengths?
Appropriate time	• When will this instruction occur? • Is there more than one time frame?
Effective instruction embedded in content	• What will you do to instruct students and prepare them for guided and independent practice? • How will you show the students or model for them?
Strategic coaching designed to support continuous growth	• Is learning progress being evidenced by the performance of each student? • How can you guide your students into independent practice based on your instruction?

- Strategic tutoring designed to support continuous growth
- Extended time for well-integrated literacy learning that moves from practice to ownership
- Ongoing informal, formative assessment of students, designed to identify how they are continuously progressing in relation to the goals of their instruction

The *students* learn in a context that supports

- Motivated and self-directed learning

- Text-based collaborative learning
- Diverse text types at a variety of difficulty levels and on a variety of topics
- Intensive writing and literacy experiences, including instruction connected to the kinds of literacy tasks that students will need to perform well in high school and beyond
- A technology component that includes technology as a tool for and a topic of literacy instruction (i.e., new literacies)

These identified instructional elements are foundational to the examples provided in this text, with a special nod toward the integration of new literacies. We do not offer how-to steps for the incorporation of fancy technological tools into language arts curriculum. Instead, we offer ideas, examples, and samples of our own dabblings and those of our students and colleagues in relation to multiple literacies. Our goals are twofold: We hope to provide insights about best instructional practices that utilize new literacies as a means to support learning for students, and we want to encourage our teaching colleagues to try some of these practices as a way to expand their own professional practices and increase their students' engagement and learning as well. In these pages, you'll find sketches and vignettes that tap into students' engagement and interest in multimodalities and multiple sign systems. Such examples help bridge classroom work to wide real-world literacy, including print, oral, gesture, and visual texts that exist in the forms of academic reading and writing, art, clothing, dance, music, and lyrics. We pay special attention to implications of such teaching for instruction that is responsive to the needs of culturally and linguistically diverse students whose primary discourses have been excluded from traditional schooling.

Through the vignettes we share throughout, we hope to illustrate the complexities of remixing or blending tried-and-true practice with current information and communication technologies, which results in a transformation of instruction that is more inclusive of all students. We feel a sense of urgency to promote this instructional transformation because of the large numbers of adolescents who are alienated by school practices and goals that they feel are outdated and unrelated to their lives (Scherff & Piazza, 2005). As a consequence, many students are not succeeding and subsequently are dropping out of high school either physically or mentally (Yagelski, 2005). Our intent is to illustrate that literacy can become a constructive yet social practice with the potential to connect and blend the experiences by which students and their teachers learn.

Remixing what is currently known about very good instruction with the engagement and learning potentials available to us through new literacies can advance learning for all students, especially those who are not currently experiencing academic success. As Biancarosa and Snow (2004) explain,

> Some 70 percent of older readers require some form of remediation. Very few of these older struggling readers need help to read the words on a page; their most common problem is that they are not able to comprehend what they read. (p. 13)

For many of these struggling students, too, a big part of the problem is that they are uninterested in what they are being assigned to read in school, because they feel it does not connect to how they are making meaning in their outside-of-school literacy worlds (Alvermann & Heron, 2001). To increase the impact of reading comprehension instruction being shared in school on student learning, the instruction must be very motivational (Guthrie & Humenick, 2004) and better unite the students' technology and literacy worlds (Moran, Ferdig, Pearson, Wardrop, & Blomeyer, 2008). The "push forward of new digital literacies and the pull backward of traditional literacy" (Labbo, 2006, p. 200) must become transparent to learners. This happens more easily as students are invited to take the lead in their learning. Using a gradual release model of instruction and learning instantiates this as a dimension of the instructional plan. Because of all of the new literacies available to students today, the distinction between the teacher and students has become blurred. In many instances, students' knowledge and enthusiasm about new technologies will allow them to take the instructional lead. Motivated, independent students—isn't this your dream come true?

Remixing the Roles of Teachers and Students

The 21st century has brought on a great shift in the way we read and write, and also in how we teach. Along with traditional forms of print-based literacy, new literacies, which are largely related to new developments in technology, occupy more and more of our daily routines and classroom practices. Just as our students have learned new literacies, so have we as we've moved from blackboards to interactive whiteboards, from overhead projectors to document cameras, from handouts to PowerPoints, from iBooks to MacBooks, from textbooks to electronic books, and from photos to YouTube clips and interactive conversations with other classrooms via Skype. One thing that educators know is that we cannot with any assurance identify the potential new technological resources that await us and our future students. For effective instruction to continue to be part of our classrooms, we must be open to these new literacies as well as the possibilities of ways in which they can enhance our teaching and our students' learning.

Although technological developments are correctly attributed to the demands of new literacies, the underlying question is how to best use these to communicate, and in doing so how to converge the in- and out-of-school literacies of our students—with the students being the primary, knowledgeable, innovative agents in this process. The shifts we see in literacy today have opened a world of possibilities for young people to actively share in reading and writing practices with others across vast spaces and experiences, which has big implications for literacy teaching and learning in school settings.

Traditionally, schools have taught reading and writing in a top-down fashion in that teachers act as experts and impart knowledge to students. This transmission model of education has been critiqued, because it forces students to take passive roles as consumers (often uncritical ones) of information (Freire, 1970). Nonetheless, this teacher-centered model of instruction remains in the mainstream and is often promoted as an efficient way to indoctrinate students of diverse backgrounds into mainstream U.S. values, Standard English, and so-called core knowledge (e.g., Hirsch, 1987; Ravitch, 2003).

Transmission models of teaching literacy are no longer relevant in a digitized world where people constantly interact with great amounts of unfiltered information. Expert knowledge must be challenged as more and more information comes from websites that are communally managed such as wikis. Today's readers have access to the work of a far more diverse group of writers than at any time in the past. In addition, connectivity allows readers to become writers in authentic contexts as they respond to what they have read. No longer the property of the few elite, the Internet has made publishing accessible for a broad spectrum of society. At the same time, because of the interactive nature of online information and the ease of online publication, even more attention to critical thinking and reading skills is necessary, because we can no longer blindly trust information sources (Eagleton & Dobler, 2007). All of this necessitates a shift in literacy instruction to emphasize students' active participation in meaning making and blurs the lines of power between teachers and students.

How Does the Gradual Release Model Support a Remixing of Instruction?

One possible shift is toward a gradual release model of learning. Think about your and your students' roles in this model as "I do it, we do it, you do it" (Fisher & Frey, 2008, p. 3). As the *I*, you begin by identifying the focus or purpose of the instruction. The purpose or lesson goal is the target you are attempting to have your students reach, such as solving an algebra problem, reading a chart of scientific information, or analyzing an author's tone and intent. The lesson purpose is shared explicitly so that students have clarity about what they should expect to accomplish as well as the instruction that will be occurring.

You'll find specific examples in all of the chapters, but for this discussion, let's draw from an example in Chapter 5 of a teacher, Jennifer Woollven, whose instructional goal was to have the students learn to write documentary poetry. She began her lesson by sharing the lesson focus or purpose when she said, "Our goal for today is to use all that we know about hip hop music as the basis for creating a form of poetry called documentary poetry." The focus can be further clarified by modeling how to think through or process the target information. As the teacher models, the students view how someone who has proficiency with the topic processes the information. This modeling, often referred to as thinking aloud (Fisher, Frey, & Lapp, 2009; Kucan & Beck, 1997), is often followed by the teacher providing guided instruction, which allows the students to work as individuals or in small groups to engage in tasks that will support their gaining an in-depth understanding of what was presented through the think-aloud.

For example, as shown in the example in Chapter 5, after Ms. Woollven stated the lesson purpose, she modeled identifying a multivoiced style to convey themes of diversity, responsibility, tolerance, and identity in Tim Swain's spoken word poem "Why I Write" (n.d.). Then she invited students to practice this level of analysis in small groups as they read other poems. While they worked, Ms. Woollven circulated among them to offer instructional supports as needed. Once the teacher feels comfortable that the students have the information needed to apply or transfer the new information, she encourages them to extend their new knowledge to a novel situation. Again using the example in Chapter 5, once Ms. Woollven observes through assessment of students' performance that they are able to independently identify and analyze a multivoiced style in poetry, she invites them to use their new literacies knowledge to create digital poetry using computers to record audio and set their poems to images. It was then that she remixed her knowledge of new literacies and her knowledge of well-structured instruction.

We have found in our teaching that remixing thoroughly planned instruction that moves from initial teacher modeling to independent student performance is enhanced when students are encouraged to integrate their new literacies knowledge. This is well illustrated in Chapter 5 when the students in Ms. Woollven's classroom illustrated ownership of their understanding of digital poetry by creating personal multimodal digital poems using computer software programs such as iMovie and Movie Maker. The role of the teacher became blurred when these very motivated students introduced Ms. Woollven to Flash as a way to animate their videos. Ms. Woollven introduced, modeled, and supported new learning, then encouraged students to use their repertoire of new literacies knowledge, which motivated them to take ownership of their learning.

In this chapter, we've discussed some of the ways that literacy is changing in the 21st century and the implications this holds for education. Although traditional literacy instruction that focuses primarily on print-based reading and writing is still vital for our students, it is insufficient given the multiple literacy demands of today's society. Thus, a remixing of "old" and "new" literacies has been deemed important and necessary for students in our schools. However, this may seem like a daunting demand for many of us who are still wondering what exactly this will look like and how to acquire the background and skills to teach in such a way.

Using the gradual release model of remixed literacies throughout this text, we share initial instructional templates designed to support your gaining or expansion of insights and expertise about how to integrate new literacies into your instruction. Our purpose is that you will move far beyond the examples we provide; we do not intend these examples to be prescriptive but rather to serve as models to help you support your remixing, understand all of the knowledge you bring to each remixing task, and gain insight about the next steps for instruction as well as your personal professional development. Table 3 is also only intended as a template, because following a checklist does not connote effective instruction (Deschler, Palincsar, Biancarosa, & Nair, 2007). Instead, we illustrate attending to students' interests and needs through motivating context.

We hope the examples we share plus the work of others (Black, 2005; Dowdall, 2006; Merchant, 2001; Zhang, 2009) will ease your worries that the literacies students draw on to compose socially will lessen their literacy prowess at school. Instead, we want to show you how these literacies can strengthen and motivate students' academic literacies and their abilities to work with others on shared tasks (Engeström, 2008). Thus, we have remixed what educators know about effective instruction with the social, collaborative, motivating forms through which adolescent students currently share their ideas, secure information, and post their communications. It is this remixing that will make transparent to learners the boundaries of their social and academic literacies. This remixing will enhance each student's learning, engagement, motivation, and performance.

We hope the lesson examples we provide support your attempts to continually expand your views of literacy instruction in ways that seamlessly remix dimensions of the best practices of your validated expertise with the new literacies emerging through online, networked environments. The end result will be students who are motivated, better equipped, and open to using many sources to find, evaluate, synthesize, utilize, create, and share new learning as well as technologies.

CHAPTER 2

Getting Started With Remix in the Classroom

This song is Copyrighted in U.S., under Seal of Copyright #154085, for a period of 28 years, and anybody caught singin' it without our permission, will be mighty good friends of ourn, cause we don't give a dern. Publish it. Write it. Sing it. Swing to it. Yodel it. We wrote it, that's all we wanted to do.

Woody Guthrie

Have you ever been invited to a social event and wondered what to wear? As a solution, did you select a belt from one outfit, a jacket from another, and a scarf or tie that had received many compliments when worn before to create a new outfit? If you are like many of us who manipulate parts of existing outfits to create new ones, you have a basic understanding of the concept of remixing in order to create something new.

Although the term *remix* is used with more frequency today, even to describe a popular soft drink and a regular column in the *New York Times Magazine*, you may still be wondering about its meaning. The term *remix* refers to the use, combination, and manipulation of cultural artifacts to create something new (Knobel & Lankshear, 2008) and was most commonly associated with music until recently. Wikipedia (n.d.) defines remix as

> an alternative version of a song, different from the original version...A remixer uses audio mixing to compose an alternate master recording of a song, adding or subtracting elements, or simply changing the equalization, dynamics, pitch, tempo, playing time, or almost any other aspect of the various musical components. (para. 1)

This style of generating new pieces from the manipulation of other audio material is frequently associated with hip-hop music (Mahiri, 2004), but the use of preexisting music to craft new music has been an integral part of creation for artists in many genres. Folk icon Woody Guthrie, for example, famously borrowed melodies from traditional church hymns to accompany lyrics he wrote for his not-so-traditional ballads.

At present, remix has come to be seen as a form of meaning making that extends beyond music and includes many other creative endeavors. In this vein, Keller (2008) considers remix as a natural part of creation: "Human culture is always derivative, and music perhaps especially so. New art builds on old art. We hear music, process it, reconfigure it, and create something derivative but new" (p. 135). Although Keller refers to music in her example, she points to the idea that all human culture is derivative and therefore remixes old cultural materials and builds upon them to create new ones.

The idea that all culture is a remix is further explored by Lessig, who argues that all culture is a remix, because humans interpret meanings through every social action, such as talking, reading, and writing, each time we respond to a text produced by others (Knobel & Lankshear, 2008). Here *text* can be broadly construed to any and all meaning-making practices. This broad understanding of remix parallels social constructivist learning theory in which learners, through interactions with others, incorporate new knowledge by building on prior knowledge (Vygotsky, 1978). This view is corroborated by hip-hop artist Daddy-O, who discusses how the practice of sampling—taking a portion of one or more songs or other sources and using it in another—relates to learning (Rose, 1994). He states, "We learn a lot from sampling, it's like school for us. When we sample a portion of a song and repeat it over and over we can better understand the matrix of the song" (Rose, 1994, p. 79).

There are many great examples of artists using the technique of sampling, and you are probably familiar with some. In case you are unfamiliar with remixing and would like to hear an example, we recommend searching YouTube for "The Grey Video" (Danger Mouse, n.d.), which mixes clips from The Beatles' film *A Hard Day's Night* (Shenson & Lester, 1964) with scenes of Jay-Z rapping the song "Encore" (Carter & West, 2003, track 4). The video fuses the two together to tell a new story that includes Ringo Starr scratching and John Lennon break dancing. The song was created by Danger Mouse, who made an entire album called *The Grey Album* (Danger Mouse, 2004) by mixing The Beatles' album *The Beatles* (also known as "The White Album"; The Beatles, 1968) with Jay-Z's *The Black Album* (Jay-Z, 2003). Another fun example is *Our Favorite Things* (Negativland, 2007), which is a DVD by the band Negativland that samples from the movie *The Sound of Music* (Wise, 1965).

While many deem remix a creative process, especially in music, to others it is believed to be a glorified form of stealing intellectual property. Indeed, many artists have been sued for their use of copyrighted materials. Not everyone shares the generosity with their work as Woody Guthrie exhibited in the quote that began this chapter. We argue that remix is quite creative in that authors thoughtfully recycle bits and pieces of many texts to cobble together new meanings. The collage-like use of preexisting texts is strategic and helps to situate the new piece within certain collective emotional, political, spiritual, or other milieus, which often means selecting appropriate visual, auditory, and other textual fragments that will resonate with others in specific ways for the purpose of guiding people to certain feelings, thoughts, and conclusions.

Situating one's work within a broader body of work is often a necessary component of writing. In academic writing, authors cite sources that have influenced their ideas and even include quotes from others to support and contextualize arguments. We see remix as akin to referencing others' material for purposes of contextualizing and building upon prior meanings. We require our students to acknowledge the sources of their information when it is possible to do so and believe that this practice not only pays proper respect to the people whose ideas each author has built upon but also helps students understand the social construction of meaning making. In other words, no ideas or writing come in a vacuum, and it is beneficial to consider how we are interdependent. On a pragmatic note, if you are concerned about the limits of copyright laws and fair use policies regarding schoolwork, you can get detailed information from the "Code of Best Practices in Fair Use for Media Literacy Education" of the National Council of Teachers of English (NCTE; 2008), which is available online.

Research on new literacies has shown that schools have been slow to incorporate new literacies practices into daily classroom instruction (Coiro, Knobel, Lankshear, & Leu, 2008; Kist, 2005). We believe it is important for classroom teachers to explore ways to bridge curriculum to outside-of-school literacy practices that are becoming more and more prevalent in the lives of our students. We also believe that teachers will be more likely to incorporate such practices if they are given a framework from which to begin their explorations. As we have stated earlier, we do not wish to send the message that new literacies can or should be reduced to simple lesson recipes. The example in the next section demonstrates how we plan new literacies lessons that bridge to traditional literacy goals. We hope this example will help demystify the process and encourage you to embark on your own lesson planning to remix traditional literacy practices with new ones.

Planning a Lesson Involving Remix

As we begin to plan a literacy lesson involving remix, we refer back to the considerations in Table 3 introduced in Chapter 1. Table 3 provides an overall picture of the elements we need to include from the lesson's inception through the assessment of student learning. Although Table 3 does not offer specifics for how to teach the lesson, it provides general guidance on issues of preparation, implementation, and evaluation of the lesson. In what follows, we will describe the process of 10th-grade teacher Mike Altamarano as he plans a literacy lesson involving the remix practice of sampling.

Generating an Idea

Like any good teacher, Mr. Altamarano hopes to incorporate new learning in ways that can tap the interests and prior knowledge of his students. He has learned about remix and understands that it is frequently used in popular music. After exploring the concept with a quick search of the Internet, he learns that sampling is a type of remix that incorporates parts of other textual material, usually songs, into a new piece. He recognizes this form as something present in a good deal of music that is popular among students.

Mr. Altamarano sees an opportunity here to create a space for students' popular music and other popular texts and tie it to school-based curricular objectives. Given that adolescence is a time when many students become alienated with school, he pays particular care to try to design lessons that will tap students' interests. He believes his lesson, which connects popular music to school literacy goals and allows space for students to draw on their out-of-school literacy knowledge and their interests, will prove engaging, even for those who may be reluctant readers and writers.

In addition to knowing his students and their interests, it is important for Mr. Altamarano to be familiar with the curricular goals relating to the content areas he teaches. He sees a parallel between the use of sampling in popular music and the use of multiple sources to synthesize information and create new meanings when writing research reports on any topic. His goal is to design a lesson that explores the notion of sampling and asks students to use the form to create their own texts.

Connecting to Standards

We know that it is not enough to design lessons that are merely "fun" or because they will keep students busy. We need to be strategic about what we teach and how we teach it. Although curricular standards sometimes feel oppressive and top-down, especially when considered in relation to the pressures of high-stakes standardized tests, the standards do reflect the broad goals of our content area instruction. Additionally, most standards provide room for the innovation and creativity necessary for teaching and learning. Therefore, we recognize the importance of identifying and connecting to appropriate standards in our lessons.

The lesson ideas throughout this book have been based on the *Standards for the English Language Arts* (International Reading Association [IRA] & NCTE, 1996). These standards parallel those used in local school districts. In the lesson that follows, Mr. Altamarano focuses his objectives on teaching students how to (a) make connections in reading and writing, (b) apply a wide range of strategies, (c) draw on prior experience and personal interactions and interpretations, and (d) use varied technological tools and resources to gather and synthesize information and communicate meaning.

For the purposes of this book, we concentrate on language arts objectives. However, it should be noted that new literacies instruction can and should permeate the entire curriculum. For example, you might notice that there is a great deal of social studies content infused in many of the example lessons we present. Readers may be interested in developing integrated lessons that also explicitly connect to social studies or other content standards.

Gathering Materials and Resources

Next, Mr. Altamarano considers what resources are available and the materials he'll use in his lesson. He already located websites that provide background information about sampling and specific examples of music that incorporate this technique. He spends some time browsing the information and selects a few songs that he believes represent his students' interests and tastes and also demonstrate diversity within the genre. For this lesson on sampling, he selects "I'll Be Missing You" (Sting, Gaither, & Evans, 1997, track 16) recorded by hip-hop artist Sean Combs under the name Puff Daddy, "All Summer Long" (King et al., 2007, track 3) recorded by rock artist Kid Rock, and *Yes We Can* (will.i.am, Jurkovac, & Dylan, 2008), a video found on YouTube by will.i.am of the Black Eyed Peas. In addition, Mr. Altamarano includes Barack Obama's political speech given after the Democratic primary of New Hampshire in 2008 and Franklin D. Roosevelt's first presidential inaugural address, both of which he also finds on the Internet.

Finally, Mr. Altamarano asks students to bring in song lyrics or transcripts of other texts from any sources that are meaningful to them. Potential examples might include popular music, television, political speeches, book quotes, movie quotes, and video games. For the sharing of songs, he uses YouTube. To get written copies of song lyrics and political speeches, he simply locates them via a quick search on Google. Computers with access to the Internet will be needed throughout the lesson.

Lesson Procedure

As in any other lesson, we must consider the steps that will be involved when we present the material in class. Here Mr. Altamarano uses the common format of the gradual release to scaffold student learning and ensure appropriate support for all students. First, he'll introduce the lesson goals and model for students. Next, he'll guide students in practice with the new material, and finally students will use the knowledge in more independent ways. Assessment will be ongoing and must link back to the goals and objectives of the lesson.

Introducing the Lesson

For this lesson, Mr. Altamarano introduces the concept in a group discussion. Because he is convinced that his students are familiar with sampling as a form of remix, even if they do not necessarily know the term, he initiates the lesson with a discussion of the meaning of sampling. Students are asked to discuss their understanding of it and provide examples of popular songs or other popular texts that incorporate the technique. In case the students are unable to think of a definition or examples, Mr. Altamarano comes prepared with his own:

> *Sampling:* A technique used in some music and other sources. It refers to the practice of borrowing portions of songs or other audio material to use in the creation of a new text.

> *Examples:* Each of the following examples was found on YouTube, and you can decide if you wish to include a "reading" of the video along with the audio:
> > • *"I'll Be Missing You"* (recorded by Puff Daddy; Sting et al., 1997): This song is a tribute to a friend of Sean Combs's who was murdered. It creates a tone of sadness and hope associated with funerals through the use of sampling from the traditional

church hymn "I'll Fly Away" (Brumley, 1929). In addition, it incorporates samples from "Every Breath You Take" (Sting, 1983, track 7) by The Police. After hearing the song, students can comment on how the two sampled songs along with the lyrics of Combs work together to create a melancholy yet hopeful reflection on the death of a friend.

- *"All Summer Long"* (recorded by Kid Rock; King et al., 2007): This song depicts the singer's reminiscences of his teenage romances during the summer of 1989. The artists sample from Warren Zevon's "Werewolves of London" (Marinell, Wachtel, & Zevon, 1978, side 1 track 4) and Lynyrd Skynyrd's "Sweet Home Alabama" (King, Rossington, & Van Zant, 1974, side 1 track 1). The inclusion of these songs contextualizes the piece within the rock genre and creates a nostalgic feeling for the music of the era being depicted in the narrative. Students can speculate about Kid Rock's target audience and discuss how the sampled songs help convey the feelings of the singer.

Getting Deeper Into Sampling

Now the concept has been defined and the students have briefly discussed the use of sampling in two examples. The next example that Mr. Altamarano shares is a music video that samples from a political speech. The video, *Yes We Can* (will.i.am et al., 2008), by artist will.i.am is a remix of Barack Obama's speech following the 2008 presidential primaries in New Hampshire. All of the words in the video are quotes taken directly from Obama's speech and especially highlight the campaign slogan, "Yes we can." Interestingly, the slogan is reminiscent of, and perhaps a "sample" from, the United Farm Workers' slogan "Sí, se puede." The video includes simple guitar music in the background and features celebrities echoing Obama's words in a call-and-response style.

Before watching the video, students are given printed copies of the Obama speech, so they can visually see how the artists cut and pasted key phrases and lines, as well as repeated the phrase "yes we can" throughout the text. As the class watches the video and follows along on the speech transcript, Mr. Altamarano uses a think-aloud strategy to discuss how the artists communicated a message of unity and hope among diverse people through their use of sampling and multivoiced echoing of the sampled words.

Practicing Together

For the next portion of the lesson, Mr. Altamarano guides students as they collaboratively design their own remix using the will.i.am video as a mentor text. First, students read from a transcript of Franklin D. Roosevelt's first inaugural address in which he famously stated that "the only thing we have to fear is fear itself." As students read, Mr. Altamarano may play an audio podcast of Roosevelt speaking, which can be found on the Internet. Periodically, Mr. Altamarano stops the reading to engage in thinking aloud. He highlights certain lines that he deems powerful and eloquent. Explaining why the wording is particularly meaningful to him, he makes specific references to the many parallels between the issues Roosevelt was addressing during the Great Depression and the economic hardships that faced the United States in 2009. For example, when Roosevelt mentions that "the withered leaves of industrial enterprise lie on every side," Mr. Altamarano might connect to the current rate of job loss and the bankruptcy of the major automobile industry companies. Similarly, when Roosevelt speaks of "money changers [that] have fled from their high seats in the temple of our civilization," Mr. Altamarano might mention the collapse of the stock market and the many examples of corporate greed that led to banks folding. As he makes these connections, he can discuss how specific images he would select to accompany the words from the speech would add to the meaning he was trying to convey. For example, in reference to corporate greed, he reminds students of the many images in the media that depict corporate bailouts, such as AIG, and people like Bernard Madoff who have come to symbolize the crisis.

As the class continues to read the entire speech, Mr. Altamarano solicits student input to assist him in selecting certain powerful lines and refrains that could be included in their videos as well as potential current images to make the connection explicit. For example, the line in the speech that reads, "only a foolish optimist can deny the dark realities of the moment," is a powerful wake-up call to those who would ignore the seriousness of the economic situation of 2009. The students offer thoughts about images that paint a picture of hardships, such as houses being foreclosed upon and people who have been laid off and wait in long lines for potential job opportunities. These images are abundant in the news and easily accessed using an Internet search on a search engine such as Google. He is careful to continually remind his students of the necessity of properly citing all sources they use, including images and other material they find on the Internet.

Mr. Altamarano then guides the class in a discussion of the underlying theme of hope and determination for unity among people for the common good. Then they discuss possible songs from popular music that would support this theme and add to the general feeling of enduring hardship, unity of people, and conquering challenges. Mr. Altamarano might suggest a song like Bob Marley and the Wailers' "Get Up, Stand Up" (Marley & Tosh, 1990, track 6), which communicates a message of civic responsibility and social agency.

Finally, Mr. Altamarano leads the students as they pull the highlighted lines from the Roosevelt text and compose them into a "poem." Figure 1 presents an example of what it might look like. The poem could then be recorded as an audio track along with the various visual images they discussed during the reading and the supporting background music to make a digital video similar to the one created by the *Yes We Can* artists. Please note that to actually create the video is quite an ambitious project and would require a good deal of class time. For the purposes of this lesson, we believe it would suffice to simply discuss the idea.

Figure 1. Franklin Roosevelt's First Inaugural Address Remixed

This is preeminently the time to speak the truth, the whole truth, frankly and boldly.
Nor need we shrink from honestly facing conditions in our country today.
This great Nation will endure as it has endured, will revive and will prosper...let me
    assert my firm belief that the only thing we have to fear is fear itself.
We face our common difficulties...government of all kinds if faced by serious
    curtailment of income...the withered leaves of industrial enterprise lie on every
    side...the savings of many years in thousand of families are gone.
More important, a host of unemployed citizens face the grim problem of existence,
    and an equally great number toil with little return.
Only a foolish optimist can deny the dark realities of the moment.
The money changers have fled from their high seats in the temple of our
    civilization. We may now restore that temple to the ancient truths. The measure
    of restoration lies in the extent to which we apply social values more noble than
    mere monetary profit.
Happiness lies not in the mere possession of money; it lies in the joy of
    achievement, in the thrill of creative effort. The joy and moral stimulation of
    work no longer must be forgotten in the mad chase of evanescent profits.
Restoration calls, however, not for changes in ethics alone. This Nation asks for
    action, and action now.
In the field of world policy I would dedicate this Nation to the policy of the good
    neighbor...the neighbor who respects his obligations and respects the sanctity
    of his agreements in and with a world of neighbors.
We now realize as we have never realized before our interdependence on each
    other...we can not merely take but we must give as well...
This great Nation will endure as it has endured, will revive and will prosper...let me
    assert my firm belief that the only thing we have to fear is fear itself.
The only thing we have to fear is fear itself.
The only thing we have to fear is fear itself.

On Their Own

For the next phase of the lesson, Mr. Altamarano has students practice the technique of sampling using sources they have selected on their own. Students are instructed to gather sources such as song lyrics, quotes from books (fiction or nonfiction), political speeches, television shows, and movies. For students who are unfamiliar with how to find such information on the Internet, he assists them in gathering materials.

The main criterion for the selection of the sources is that they hold meaning for the students. This could mean that they love the source materials, dislike them, or simply that they are reminders of something. Students then follow the same procedure they did in the lesson with Mr. Altamarano. First, they reread the selected text and underline keywords and phrases that resonate with them. Next, students reconfigure the phrases into a new piece of writing. As in the examples shared at the beginning of the lesson, the sampling does not have to comprise the entire text nor is it necessary to include visual images. Instead, students may sample small bits of text and intersperse their own writing around the textual samples, as did the artists in the songs "I'll Be Missing You" and "All Summer Long" mentioned earlier in this chapter. In these cases, the samples serve to situate and bolster the meaning of the student-authors' texts but do not overshadow them.

Continual Performing Assessment

As is the case with any lesson, you must consider how you'll know if students are learning the new material and how well they're incorporating the information into their repertoire of practice. Assessment must connect to the goals and objectives of the lesson. During each phase of the lesson, monitor student work and check for comprehension. We find it helpful to be explicit about our objectives up front so that students are aware of what is expected from them.

In the case of Mr. Altamarano's lesson, his goals related to students' learning about the technique of sampling as a way to comprehend, interpret, and evaluate texts. This includes connecting their own prior knowledge to new texts and using a variety of sources to synthesize information and create new meaning. As students analyze texts that incorporate sampling and then use the technique to create their own texts, students demonstrate an understanding of how textual meaning builds on the work of others. In other words, all writing is a form of remix. The writing work samples created by each student reflect their understanding of the lesson objectives and can be used by Mr. Altamarano for assessment purposes.

Moving Forward

The sampling lesson described in this chapter is meant to give a detailed account of how we start our lesson designs to incorporate remix in the classroom. The sampling lesson took a quite literal approach to remix by borrowing directly from the popular music industry's use of the term. The lesson ideas that follow in the next chapters illustrate many ways we can incorporate this same idea (remix) but in different ways. Our goal and intention is to open space in the classroom for new literacies practices while maintaining a strong base in traditional literacy practices. We contend that this is not only possible but also that the two complement each other. We believe that other work being done in the area of new literacies also demonstrates this same goal.

Given our desire to make our work accessible and useful to teachers who may not have a great deal of experience in "new" literacies but are certainly well versed in the traditional ones, we have organized the remaining three chapters around three big areas commonly associated with literacy development: speaking, reading, and writing. However, recognizing that these are reciprocal processes that can't really be teased apart—nor should they be—each chapter has overlap in terms of the foci.

CHAPTER 3

Say It Well: Remixing Oral Discourse and New Literacies Instruction

"When I use a word," Humpty Dumpty said in rather a scornful tone, "it means just what I choose it to mean— neither more nor less."

"The question is," said Alice, "whether you can make words mean so many different things."

"The question is," said Humpty Dumpty, "which is to be master—that's all."

Lewis Carroll

Think about a typical day in your life. In how many conversations do you participate? Do you change your style, vocabulary, and tone depending on your intent and relationship with the others involved in the conversation? If you're able to move easily among many language communities, you're linguistically versatile. This may or may not be the case for many of your students who come to school speaking the languages they've learned in their homes, "as they actively participate in culturally defined systems of practices such as participating in religious classes, playing sports or games, and participating in formal and non-formal schooling practices" (Gutiérrez, Baquedano-Lopez, & Turner, 1997, p. 369).

Before entering school, children have four to five years to practice meaningful interactions with the other members of their home and neighborhood language communities. In many of these social-conversational exchanges, the children are positioned as the center of the conversations. Such experiences afford them opportunities to try on language, which has been reinforced with hugs, restatements, and content extensions. Through these early language experiences, children begin to believe that language interchanges happen communally, most of the time positively, and definitely with purpose. These early experiences with language expose them to what Halliday (1994) refers to as the ideational and intentional functions of language. Halliday's insights suggest that it is the intent of the speaker to purposely share content through the words chosen and the manner in which they are delivered. For example, a parent verbally disciplining a child extends a message that has different content and intention than when the child is being verbally applauded or encouraged by the same adult.

During these early years, children are socialized to the nuances of their language or discourse communities (Gee, 1996). Children enter the community of the classroom and encounter a new language community, although they bring with them this set of personal language experiences. For many students, even those who are native English speakers, this new school language community is not similar to what they've experienced in their homes. Not only do students encounter a change of lexicon or vocabulary and content but also the intention, which is now to share a great deal of information with many, is also unfamiliar. Often not the center of interactions, how students are newly and continually positioned and addressed in the school interactions affects their views of themselves (Delpit, 1988). When issues of power and language are not explicitly addressed in schooling, many students from marginalized Discourse communities feel a sense of alienation with school learning (Delpit & Dowdy, 2002). This alienation often grows as students progress in age.

Is Adding the Discourse of School the Same for Everyone?

On playgrounds throughout the United States, the chant "sticks and stones may break my bones but words will never hurt me" is often heard. Unfortunately for many students, the message of the chant does not ring true. Words, the way they are spoken, and by whom have the power to support or destroy one's self-perception and subsequent learning. To fully realize this, think about what you inferred your teachers thought about you as a learner. Did you determine this from expressed words, tones, or gestures? What was spoken? How did the teachers speak? What was implied? How so? Who was the audience? Did you believe it then, and even more, to emphasize the power of the teacher's voice, do you still believe it? In most instances, what was said became your reality and a part of your identity. Do you carry those identities with you today? Did you learn early that you had wonderful ideas, were a terrific writer, could solve a math problem easily, or captured the intended message of an author? Or did you learn that you took too long to respond, you procrastinated, and if you only tried harder, you would "get it"? We encourage you to reflect on the feelings and learning that were evoked from these interactions and then to realize always the power your language has to support or destroy each of your students' potential for engagement, learning, and success.

What Characterizes School Talk?

Research suggests that school talk, or academic English characterized as the language used by teachers to support their students' acquisition and sharing of new academic knowledge, information, skills, and abstract ideas (Chamot & O'Malley, 1989), is often closely aligned with the discourse communities of white students and those of high socioeconomic status. Students of color and those from working-class and economically marginalized backgrounds often experience a mismatch between their cultures and languages and the academic language experienced at school (Hart & Risley, 1995; Heath, 1983, 1991). One area in which this mismatch often manifests is spoken language, because many students come from homes and communities where members speak languages and dialects other than Standard English, which is the language favored in schools and viewed there as the prestigious language, because it is the primary one spoken by the powerful of the country (Smitherman, 2000; Wolfram, Adger, & Christian, 1999). Realizing that many students need to add a school discourse, what then happens at school is very crucial, and the role we have as educators in supporting language growth is of paramount importance to every student's success.

Acquiring School Talk as an Additive Discourse

The power of one's language has been studied by educational researchers who largely agree that learning Standard English is important for social mobility, because it represents communication within the codes of power (Delpit, 1995; González, Moll, & Amanti, 2004; Gutiérrez & Lee, 2009), tells the world what a person knows (Marzano, 2004), and enables judgments about one's intelligence (Stahl, 2005). Having the language needed for every situation empowers the speaker to be acknowledged, accepted, and understood.

However, the ability to use Standard or academic English in appropriate contexts should not require a rejection of other registers that may even be students' home languages, such as African American Vernacular English, code-switching between English and Spanish, and a working-class, white, Southern dialect (Deschenes, Cuban, & Tyack, 2001; Lee, 2006). In fact, many linguists and educators have long noted that nonstandard forms of English are equally as complex as Standard English and just as useful in the expression of ideas, depending on the context (Ball & Farr, 2003; Edwards, 2007; Hymes, 1972; Labov, 1972; Smitherman, 1977). Today, especially with the Internet and other technologies that have resulted in a more connected and "shrinking" world, nonstandard forms of English are increasingly prevalent in mainstream society (The New London Group, 1996). This expanded understanding of communication invites instruction that better blends students' home and school languages (Brock, Lapp, Salas, & Townsend, 2009; Turner, 2009).

Schools and teachers need to be prepared to provide learning exchanges that ensure that the acquisition of school talk happens in a positive, instructionally supportive environment where the students' home languages are seen as powerful bases for acquiring future learning (Johnston, 2004; Swadener, 1995). An additive model of language development becomes a reality for every student when teachers speak to them as valued, intelligent, productive members of a very important community—the classroom community. In this atmosphere, the languages children bring to school are seen as a significant and appropriate base that can be used to add the discourse of school talk. We believe that if teachers are taught how to share a model of additive language, they will.

We do not intend to place a value judgment on one form of expression over another. Instead, we propose that students, who are exposed to many varieties of oral language as a means of expression, need to be encouraged to use these oral discourses as tools for effectively communicating as they move among the communities of their lives. We contend that students must learn to value multiple means of expression and should be able to skillfully utilize different oral discourses, depending on the specific contexts in which they are communicating. We believe that with appropriate in-school support, students will learn to value and feel confidence and pride in their abilities to navigate diverse communicational contexts. We further believe that the first step in offering students this support is for this goal to be foregrounded in the instructional behaviors of every teacher. We hope that most teachers will gladly accept this challenge if they are offered the appropriate professional development. We intend this chapter and book as one means to this end.

Supporting an Additive Model of Language Development

To achieve the goal of presenting an additive model of language, we must first help students identify the sociopolitical nature of how language works in our society. We believe this is something that has been largely left out of traditional schooling, which tends to privilege Standard English above all other forms of communication. Additionally, we believe teachers can guide students to become sociologists and anthropologists of a sort by investigating and exploring the diverse oral discourses they find around them. Are you wondering what expertise is needed to begin this instruction? We contend that teachers need not be experts in all styles of communication present in and around their classrooms. Instead, with our students, we can engage in dialogic inquiry as we explore how language functions to express meaning and even embody power. In such a classroom environment, teachers and students share expert status in this collaborative inquiry.

Identifying the Range of Possibilities

The range of language contexts in which students function in a typical school day are well described by Bailey and Heritage (2008), who identify the two primary macrostructures of language function as social language and academic language. Social language, which involves daily informal, mostly face-to-face oral exchanges with friends, family, peers, and colleagues, is often one's primary mode of communication. Additional exchanges of social language, or networking, are conveyed via new literacies as students communicate while text messaging or interacting on iChat, Skype, and Internet sites similar to Facebook and MySpace. Bailey and Heritage (2008) also identify school navigational language and curriculum content language as the two primary categories within academic language.

Language of School Routines

Navigational language includes the many commands or instructions teachers offer, such as "get into your book clubs" or "put everything away before going to lunch." However, this mostly oral communication is continued by students when they say, for example, "take the ball to the court when you're ready" and "take notes on this and I'll take notes on that." School navigational language supports one's participation in daily school rituals. We believe that this can carry over to the home where students and their families direct each other's successful navigation.

Language of the School Curriculum

A second type of academic language, curriculum content language, requires being able to understand the language of oral and written curriculum content, which is often densely packed with meaning and many abstract and technical vocabulary terms. This is the most formal of the language types, and like other language functions, individuals' levels of competency are related to prior experiences with it. For example, students who come from homes where a less formal discourse style is always present may not feel comfortable or be able to comprehend fully— or may take an oppositional stance toward either school navigational or content-specific language. Providing students with the tools to engage with formal academic language is important but not enough. Making space and resources available for students to engage with multiple discourses and critically analyze them from a sociocultural standpoint helps students comprehend the enormous power that words hold in the lives of all people.

Implementing an Additive Model of Language Development in the Classroom

The instructional examples outlined in this chapter are designed to model how to help students expand the messages and the delivery of the messages shared through their vocalized language as they read the multiple texts they have around them and then use this information to create new meanings via the new literacies in which most are very interested. When students have proficiency with the academic structures of English, they should be able to understand the explanations offered by their teachers who are sharing content from many disciplines, read from multiple sources, discuss what they are learning, and convey ideas about their learning through written formats. As we mentioned in Chapter 1, due to the page limitations of this book, we cannot share every detail of each of these lesson examples. Our primary goal instead is to illustrate how the teachers remixed their bases of knowledge and also how the students were encouraged to remix and expand their literacies.

Although a number of the English language arts standards of IRA and NCTE (1996) are addressed in these lessons, the lessons focus most prominently on teaching students how to use spoken, written, and visual language (e.g., strategies, conventions, style, vocabulary) to communicate effectively with a variety of audiences and for different purposes. Before we proceed to the lesson examples, it is important to note that some of the issues we address, and that you may subsequently present to your students, run the risk of appearing to be stereotyping and therefore may need to be discussed with your students. Stereotyping can occur, because oral discourses are often demarcated by sociocultural constructs like race, ethnicity, class, and geography. When we begin to identify discourses, it could be inferred that one is essentializing people from different groups and generalizing certain characteristics to all members. In your initial discussions with your students, you may wish to note first that this is not your intent. Yet, when one thinks about this more fully, it becomes clear that this is almost impossible, because there is great diversity within all groups, even within classrooms.

Second, nobody fits neatly into just one group. Clearly, people can be members of a variety of different groups and have influences from many groups, and therefore simplistic attempts to classify people into discourse communities are doomed to failure and can be insulting. We do not wish to fall into this trap, nor do we wish to advocate for you to teach lessons that lead to such ends. Therefore, it is of the utmost importance to proceed with caution when asking students to investigate, identify, and utilize various forms of oral discourse for school purposes. All lessons in which students explore oral discourse should allow for them to discuss and represent the complexity and interconnectedness of differing discourses as well as the arbitrary and socially constructed nature of the value judgments assigned to them in mainstream society.

New Literacies and Language Connections

Technology such as the Internet has expanded the access that ordinary people have to multiple forms of texts, many of which are unfiltered by professional editors. On one hand, this has broadened the potential for people from diverse communities to be exposed to and even interact with others from distinct groups they may not have encountered prior to the explosion of Web 2.0–type changes. On the other hand, as Leu and colleagues (2004) have noted, many students are unaware of the importance of critical evaluation while reading online—or in any context, for that matter. Given the broadened access and diverse possibilities of texts students read and create, the following lessons further model how to incorporate multimodal text forms to help students gain multiple tools to express their ideas in diverse, critical, and thoughtful ways and also critically evaluate information and information sources.

These examples also illustrate an additive model of language expansion, which supports both teachers and students by drawing from their diverse Discourses to remix information for communicative purposes. This occurs through continual, purposeful conversations in which teachers do the following:

- Model the academic language appropriate to the content topic within the context of gaining an understanding of the targeted material. This happens as the "teacher questions her own assumptions, acknowledges ethical dilemmas hidden in her position, refers to inconvenient theories, facts, and philosophies that she has deliberately overlooked and demonstrates an openness to alternative viewpoints" (Brookfield, 1995, p. 19).

- Invite students within a variety of collaborative configurations to try on the newly encountered words, structures, and concepts. Language and its many uses positively permeate the instructional day.

- Model and promote posing and answering higher-level questions. Invitations to think and question aloud are genuinely modeled by teachers and accepted by students in content classrooms that support an additive model of language expansion.

- Promote comparatively analyzing a wide array of texts. All of the teacher's behaviors, all day long, serve as a model for students. When the teacher questions the premises of one author and then compares these to the voices of other authors, students are encouraged to analyze and personally debate multiple perspectives.

- Offer restatements and extensions of the content information because of insights gained from observing student performance. By orally restating, summarizing, synthesizing, comparing, and extending newly learned information, teachers have an opportunity to model academic language and literacy strategies throughout the day.

- Support students as they move to independence through describing, explaining, clarifying, questioning, mitigating, evaluating, and communicating their thoughts and feelings about the targeted content topics and processes. We know our students by observing their performance. With this knowledge, we are able to plan the next steps in our teaching and their learning experiences.

Lesson Example 1: School Montage

In film, montage is a technique that refers to a rapid sequence of scenes or images used to underscore a theme. The sequence, which condenses narrative, is achieved through editing. In U.S. film, this technique has been used primarily to advance the story while suggesting the passage of time. An example can be found in the movie *Rocky* (Chartoff, Winkler, & Avildsen, 1976) when Sylvester Stallone's character goes through a strenuous training regimen to get in shape for his big fight. The passage of time is shown through a series of images of the Rocky character exercising, set to the theme song of the movie. Many students will also be familiar with the montage sequence in the movie *The Lion King* (Hahn, Allers, & Minkoff, 1994), which shows the character of Simba growing from a cub to an adult lion while music plays in the background.

Soviet montage theory, also called intellectual montage, is more symbolic. The Soviet theory uses images, often seemingly disconnected, that are juxtaposed to create new symbolic meanings in the minds of viewers. Sergei Eisenstein, a Soviet Russian film director, was known for his use of montage. He described the technique as a way to explode ideas into being by colliding images. He believed that the conflict created by forcing the intellectual comparisons of selected images paralleled everyday thought processes in people and therefore caused viewers to actually form thoughts (Pincus & Ascher, 1984).

School Montage Overview

This sequence of lessons was designed to expand student insights about how to create a literary montage. As we review the lesson sequence, note the recursiveness of the gradual release model of instruction that is being played out between the teacher and students. At times, the teacher takes the lead, whereas at other times, the teacher steps aside and supports students as they move toward independence. This becomes possible as the teacher continually observes the performance of the students and scaffolds instructional supports as needed. In this lesson, you'll notice that the teacher's goal is to have her students create a literary montage. Attainment of this goal involves the following recursive interactions between the teacher and her students.

1. Invite students to explore montage in film by first modeling and then helping them analyze examples that employ the technique. Many examples can be found on the Internet (e.g., filmplus.org/montage.html). The lesson example that follows includes some additional possibilities. (modeling and guiding instruction)

2. Invite student groups to discuss how different places in and around their school have different environments (e.g., shops, parks, homes). (collaborative learning)

3. Model for students how to use digital cameras to capture images representing the different atmospheres they identified in the previous discussion. (modeling and guiding instruction)

4. Invite students to use editing software (e.g., Movie Maker, iMovie, PowerPoint) to create montage sequences with audio soundtracks and text inserts to depict the various environments students identified in the school. This isn't as hard as it may sound, and many of your students probably already know how to do this. (transfer and independence)

5. Draw on students' prior knowledge to write narrative summaries that provide an analysis of their montages. If students are unsure of how to do so, you may need to provide a written model. (transfer and independence)

6. Act as a participant as students share and discuss their work. (independence achieved)

Learning success is achieved within a lesson when ownership is transferred from the teacher to the students. This occurs when the instruction is "organized to encourage and support a continued, increasingly mature and comprehensive acceptance of responsibility for one's own learning" (Kesten, 1987, p. 15). This gradual release from the teacher to the students through a scaffolding of information is based on Vygotsky's (1962) performance assessment notion that children can learn anything if the adult/teacher begins with what the child knows about the topic or process and then provides content, tasks, and materials that are gradually withdrawn as the child grows in independence. Notice in this example that the release by the teacher is gradual and occurs as the teacher observes the performance of the students in relation to what is being taught. As students grow in knowledge and competence, the teacher introduces new concepts and the gradual release process begins again.

School Montage in Action

The students in Laura Friedman's 10th-grade English class had been discussing various forms of communication and the many ways people express themselves in different contexts. Ms. Friedman introduces Gee's (1996) theory of primary and secondary Discourses by giving the example of her father's educational experiences during the 1940s and 1950s. First, Ms. Friedman provides a focus for the lesson, then she builds background knowledge by thinking aloud about a personal experience. You'll notice that her responses introduce the concept that language is additive. You do not have to lose but instead can add language for many contexts. Notice, too, how she supports students as they realize the importance of their language as an instructional base. In the following excerpt from a classroom discussion, she tips the power for knowledge as well as language growth to the students:

"I'm going to tell you a story about my dad. At the end, I'd like to hear your thoughts. My father was raised in a working-class, East European, Jewish enclave in South Bronx, New York. Although English was his first language, his parents, like many of the elders in the community, spoke Yiddish at home and mixed a great deal of Yiddish into their conversations even when speaking English. My dad grew up speaking English with an accent typical of his area of the Bronx during that time period. When he spoke, it was not uncommon for him to incorporate Yiddish words from his native language as a tool for expression, especially in certain contexts. Words such as *bobke, kishke, ponim,* and *shmalts* are just a few examples of the kind of vocabulary that peppered his regular speech. This was his primary discourse, or language, and it served him quite well in his community.

"When my dad went to school, he was introduced to Standard English, which is what the talk we do here at school is called. School talk became a secondary discourse for him. Although he managed to make his way through public schooling and on to City College of New York, he never lost the Bronx accent or the style of speech typical of his community. This became an obstacle for him, because he attended college in the early 1950s during the McCarthy Era, a time when diversity was frowned upon and even punished. My dad's speech was deemed un-American, and he was forced to take speech classes designed to teach him to speak "properly" and rid him of his foreign accent. He eventually passed the class and went on to graduate, although I've often questioned whether the required course had any long-term impact on his speech accent."

When she pauses, Jaime (all student names are pseudonyms) quickly says, "You mean, he never lost his accent."

"No," responds Ms. Friedman, "he never lost his accent, but he still has a wonderful vocabulary and is able to communicate with everyone. I know each of you has a language story that may be similar to my dad's, and each of us has experiences that happened as we've tried to expand our home language to include the language we hear, read, and speak at school. I'd love to have you share your language stories. Before we share as a whole class, I'd like you to cluster into groups of three to share your own stories relating to your primary, or home, and your secondary or school languages or discourses."

After chatting for a while in clusters, everyone engages in a whole-class conversation. Like many educators, Ms. Friedman finds that her adolescent students are reticent to share with the whole class before trying their ideas out on a few. After initial small cluster or partner talk, they are very willing to share with the whole class. A number of the Mexican

American students in the class share examples of ways their family incorporated Spanish into daily conversation. For example, Daniela says,

> "I don't really speak Spanish, but it's my grandparents' first language. When they were in school, they got in trouble for speaking it. They said they didn't want the same thing to happen to their kids, so they didn't speak to them in Spanish. My mom can understand it, but she doesn't speak it that much. I know some words. When my grandparents talk to each other, they switch back and forth between English and Spanish."

This leads to further discussion about the way people change their speech and even their behavior depending on the context. Note in the following excerpt how Ms. Friedman models academic language through conversational exchanges with the students. Students give examples of different ways they would tell the same story to different people. For example, Mario starts this conversation:

> "If I see a fight between students in school, I would talk about it one way to my friends, a different way to my parents, and another way if the police questioned me. I wouldn't only talk with words, I'd act differently."
>
> "Me, too," says Paola. "If the police asked me, I wouldn't tell details."
>
> "I wouldn't tell details to my dad either," laughed Julio.
>
> "Your dad is like talking to the police," added Annaleigha.
>
> "So it's not just our words that change as we talk to different people in each of these communities. It's also the nuances or characteristics of the way we present the message," Ms. Friedman notes.
>
> She continues, "Even within school, students talk and act in different ways, depending on where they are and to whom they're speaking. For example, some of you speak in an informal way when you're with friends in the cafeteria or in the halls between classes compared to when you are in class with your teachers."
>
> Anthony adds, "There are even differences in the way me and my homeboys speak and act in different classes, and that primarily depends on the teacher and who else can hear us."
>
> "Yes," says Ms. Friedman, "the atmosphere that the teacher and the students set up as a group certainly affects how you speak and act. It's so important to be able to detect these different nuances and draw from all of your behaviors and discourses to accommodate the situation."
>
> "For sure," says Gabriella, "because if you mess up, everyone thinks you're stupid."

Based on their performance, Ms. Friedman knows they're ready to move on. Reflecting and extending occurs continually throughout a lesson. As everyone shares a laugh, signaling a shared understanding of the power of language and the importance of their language use in a variety of settings, Ms. Friedman next explains that the students would be exploring different discourses and environments in their school using a technique called montage. She is aware of her students' progress and provides natural scaffolding as the lesson develops.

To build her students' background knowledge, she explains that in film, montage refers to the practice of editing together sequences of images to lead viewers to have specific thoughts—like a collage of images over time on the screen. She asks the students if they could think of any examples from movies or television where they had seen this technique employed. Some students think they've seen examples of this, but no one can remember exactly where. Ms. Friedman is attempting to build the needed background information. She does this through oral description and also by providing an actual model that the students can visualize. It is here that she begins her remixing as she incorporates a new literacy (creating a film montage) into this well-scaffolded lesson.

Because they're unable to discuss examples from memory, Ms. Friedman has students view some examples she found on the Internet. An online search using the term *montage sequence* provides further information and examples. Figure 2 gives a brief overview of an intellectual montage that can be shared with students.

After viewing a few examples to get the general idea of montage, Ms. Friedman tells the students that they will next see an example from a famous 1920s Soviet movie called *October: Ten Days That Shook the World* (Aleksandrov & Eisenstein, 1928). She explains that the film had been made to celebrate the 10th anniversary of the Soviet Revolution. Although the students did not have much background knowledge of the Soviet Revolution, Ms. Friedman plays the clip that she found on the Internet, because it provides an excellent example of juxtaposition of various powerful images and sounds. As the students watch, they use a Storyboard for a Montage Sequence (see the Appendix) as a graphic organizer to list the images they saw and the accompanying audio.

Students then discuss their interpretations of the montage sequence. Ms. Friedman guides the class discussion by asking the following questions:

- How were the different images shown in the clip connected?
- How was sound and text used to help convey meaning?
- What do you think the filmmaker was trying to say?

With this guided instruction, Ms. Friedman supports students as they build the language and concepts needed to continue their learning.

Figure 2. A Sample of an Intellectual Montage

A montage is a sequence of images that collide and explode ideas into the viewers' minds. Often, audio is used to augment the meaning being conveyed in the juxtaposed images.

In the following sequence, an image of a cow is followed by one of a hamburger. The cow alone may evoke a wide variety of thoughts, but coupled with the hamburger, the options are narrowed. Still, the viewer may have drastically different feelings inspired by the collision of these two images, depending on the viewer's attitude toward human consumption of meat or other prior experiences with fast food or farm animals.

With more images colliding in a sequence, authors can further guide viewers to the types of thinking intended. The above sequence could be augmented with the inclusion of a third image depicting death.

The inclusion of music or other sound can augment the author's intended message. With this particular sequence, somber music or frightening sound effects, as is typical in horror films, forces viewers to think about the inevitable death of the cow to make a burger.

The students comment on the fact that the images are all religious in nature. The film starts with pictures of a Christian church and a statue of Jesus, then flashes images from many other religions from around the world. The students also note that the audio track sounded like church bells, but they were ringing frantically, even violently. The students agree that this part of the film seems to be comparing different world religions, and it seems to be critical of religion. The soundtrack helps to convey the critical sentiment in the minds of the students. The second part of the montage adds to the critical feel of the sequence. In this part, the images change from religious to military. One student suggests that the filmmaker's intent might have been to show that religious differences are often the cause of wars.

Now that the students are thinking about how images are put together to create meaning in montage, Ms. Friedman shows one last example to guide the students' thinking toward the topic of schooling. She selects a brief clip from the beginning of the movie *The Breakfast Club* (Hughes & Tanen, 1985). She offers this additional example to continue the students' move to independence through conversational collaboration.

In this clip, a series of shots from a high school are edited together and accompanied by a voice-over narration by a student, who critiques the simplistic categories (i.e., brain, athlete, basket case, princess, criminal) that are used to label young people. As the voice-over mentions each of the student categories, images are cut in to represent them (computer lab, locker room, counselor's office, prom queen, graffiti on a locker). Although this is a nice example, a similar effect could be obtained through class discussion or a simple school montage made by the teacher. The important instructional feature at this point in the lesson is that the teacher is still supporting the building of a knowledge base that will move students to independence.

During a class discussion after viewing this montage sequence, Ms. Friedman guides the students' conversation by asking a series of questions, such as, How were the different images shown in the clip connected? How was audio used to convey meaning? What do you think the filmmaker was trying to say? Do you think the filmmaker presented an accurate depiction of high school students? Why or why not? In a lively discussion, students point out that the categories in the movie were somewhat contrived. However, they all agree that students in their school do form social groups around certain themes, and some of the categories found in the movie (e.g., athletes) parallel those found in their school. The students also all agreed that each group has a shared Discourse. Through this conversational give-and-take, Ms. Friedman can assess whether the students are ready to proceed independently. When she detects missing information or language, she restates it.

Ms. Friedman explains that their next task would be to use montage as a technique to represent the different discourses found in the school. Students work in small groups of two or three. Each group is given the task of using digital tools to create a montage sequence of one minute or less that juxtaposes different scenes in and around the school. She gives the groups the following instructions, and as students continue to move toward independence, she moves to the background where she can still offer support as needed:

1. First, create a map of the school with your partners. On the map, you should identify different areas where you find different discourse communities or atmospheres where people act, speak, and interact differently. Use a storyboard to plan how your images will collide

(see the Appendix for a Storyboard for a Montage Sequence template).

2. Then use digital cameras or cell phones to take pictures of different places you identified in school that represent different atmospheres. Take between five and 10 pictures of each identified area.

3. Upload your pictures onto a computer and use the editing software to cut sequences of images to compare and contrast the various atmospheres you have identified.

4. Select music that helps to convey the overall message you wish to relate and add it to the audio track to correspond with your visual images. Try to select music that helps illustrate the meanings you wish to convey about each specific context or environment. (Ask students to bring in CDs from their own music collections or make CDs and free-download websites available. Many students have experience creating their own music and other audio using programs, such as GarageBand and Audacity. This is a great way to incorporate such literacy skills for school learning—and remix your literacies.

5. Add text to the montage by creating titles for each identified area.

6. Reflect on what you've learned and write a brief narrative summary to provide analysis of your montage. Be sure to include a description of each area you identified, why you think the atmosphere exists in the way it does, and how your images and audio tracks contribute to the message you are trying to convey.

Throughout the school year, Ms. Friedman's students have opportunities to create short movies using cameras and iMovie software on the classroom computers. If this had been the first time she incorporated these tools into a lesson, she would have given more explicit directions on the technical aspects of how to use the equipment. We have found that most high school students have had some experience making digital movies. See Table 4 for websites that can help you gain background in digital tools for moviemaking.

Once students complete the activity, the class gathers to view and discuss their work, which allows students and the teacher to reflect and extend their thinking. In one group's storyboard, the issue of control is highlighted by showing different room arrangements in each frame. The images show scenes representing different classrooms the students experience each day at school. The montage juxtaposes scenes from classes that the students find engaging and other classes that they describe as

Table 4. A "How-To" for Digital Videos

- Adobe® Instructional Resources for K–12:
  www.adobe.com/education/resources/k12/instructional/
- Center for Digital Storytelling's Digital Storytelling Cookbook:
  www.storycenter.org/cookbook.pdf
- iMovie®: www.apple.com/life/imovie
- Llano Grande Center's Captura Digital Storytelling Toolkit:
  captura.llanogrande.org
- Movie Maker™: www.microsoft.com/windowsxp/using/moviemaker/default.mspx

boring. Interestingly, the images of "boring" classes all feature rows of student desks facing the front of the room, whereas the images of "engaging" classes are all of elective courses and show students involved in hands-on activities, such as playing musical instruments and practicing salsa dancing. The song this group chose for the audio track, "¿A quién le Importa?" (Berlanga & Canut, 2002), which translates to "who cares," is sung by Mexican pop star Thalía. The song describes someone who is constantly judged and criticized but shouts back "who cares." According to one of the students in the group, Brenda, they selected this particular song, "because she says what it is really like to be a teenager." During the discussion of this piece, the other students in the class agree that the environment setup in different classes often determines how students behave and interact. All of the students agree that school is boring when class is run in a lecture format, which leads to disinterest and often disruptive student behavior. On the other hand, the students claim that classes that promote hands-on types of experiences help students feel motivated and engaged in the classwork.

School Montage Wrap-Up

Having students engage in montage making based in school experiences provides Ms. Friedman a window from which to view her students' thinking about the ways in which discourses shape and are shaped by environmental factors. In addition, she can see students' analytical work as they observe, critique, and write their perceptions of schooling. The various discussions and work samples provide excellent assessment material and offer the students authentic ways to engage in school talk or discourse. Ms. Friedman finds that when students engage in montage making based on school experiences, they develop oral language through conversation and presentation as well as reading skills of synthesizing and evaluating. In addition, the writing involved in these activities ranges from reflective journaling to new literacies remixing of digital images and sounds.

A year earlier, Ms. Friedman had been skeptical about involving her students in a learning experience like creating a montage. She worried that she wouldn't be able to cover all of the standards and that the students would goof off and not stay on task. Her instruction, like that of many secondary educators, mostly involved students in a whole-class reading of a classic novel or textbook (Bean, 2000). She shared with one of her colleagues that her students were often bored with the readings, which led to a discussion about what motivates and engages high school students. Both teachers knew that their students were very interested in technology, so they decided to create learning experiences that addressed the same standards but would be of more interest to their students. They found that the more involved the students were, the more they stayed on task with the project as well as the integrated literacy aspects (i.e., reading, writing, conversing) required to complete the task. Engaged students coordinated their "strategies and knowledge within a community of literacy in order to fulfill their personal goals, desires and intentions" (Guthrie & Wigfield, 2000, p. 404). Both teachers are now convinced that when their students participate in socially constructed tasks like creating a montage, literacy learning and language expansion occur. Ms. Freidman and her colleague acknowledge that they themselves must also be continually learning to construct together a curriculum that ensures a high level of student engagement. They get many of their innovative instructional ideas from lessons presented on ReadWriteThink's website, www.readwritethink.org.

Lesson Example 2: Literary Remix

In this lesson, which we call *literary remix*, students focus on intertextual connections to build their understandings of literature situated in particular social, cultural, and historical contexts. Students communicate their understandings by creating new multimodal texts that represent ideas based in their own research. This degree of involvement results in engaged, on-task students who sharpen and expand their literacy learning through socially constructed tasks. These beliefs are also borne out by the work of many other educators (Franzak, 2006; Ivey & Broaddus, 2001, 2007; Schallert & Reed, 1997) who have found that learning is enhanced among adolescents who have "space and times that welcome the reading, discussion, and sharing of texts (and tasks) that adolescents like to read, and in particular, with an eye toward issues important to youth, such as

relationships, justice, personal struggles, and making difficult decisions"
(Ivey, 2008, p. 20).

Literary remix illustrates this high degree of engagement and learning
over a five-week time period, consisting of about 30–40 minutes per day
of instruction, learning, and sharing. All of Diane's (author) instruction is
contextualized within standards-based units of study designed by her with
input from her students about how to include new literacies and related
readings.

Literary Remix Overview

In addition to teaching at a university, Diane teaches 11th- and 12th-grade
English in an ethnically and racially diverse school. Over the years, she
has noticed that her students are highly motivated and engaged in reading
and writing when space is made in the curriculum for their collaborative
inquiry. In addition, her students respond positively when she makes an
effort to connect their language arts learning to issues that are current and
seen by them as personally relevant in their lives.

Issues of race and racism can be hot topics in classrooms, often
provoking emotional reactions on the part of students and teachers alike.
Perhaps it is for this reason that such issues are often left out of standard
curriculum. However, Diane, like a growing number of teachers,
recognizes the great importance of addressing topics that are pressing
and present in the minds of her students, even if such topics are potentially
uncomfortable at times. After observing conversations of students
that often revolved around issues of race and racism, something that
was heightened when race became a topic of national conversation in
mainstream media and other sources as a result of a historic presidential
election, she decided to design a series of learning experiences with the
primary goal being for students to understand how to examine racial
profiling through a literary lens.

This literary remix lesson was designed to expand student insights
about

- The use of flashback as a literary technique
- The important of audience in determining the voice when sharing a
  story
- The writings of authors living during the Harlem Renaissance
- The existence of racism in the lives of writers during that time period

Attainment of these goals involved the following well-scaffolded, teacher–student recursive interactions:

1. Introduce students to a particular time period, a poet within the period, themes that were expressed within the poems, and their social significance. (modeling)

2. Support students in examining one piece of work by the writer for its social and historical significance. (teacher–student collaboration)

3. Invite students to conduct library and Internet research on one or more writers from the selected time period and then contrast their topically related messages. This helps students build their background knowledge, language bases, and understanding of different perspectives. (teacher–student collaboration)

4. Ask students to "introduce" the writers by orally presenting essays that focus on the backgrounds, beliefs, accomplishments, and personal histories of the selected writers. The presentations are set to music, which is selected by the students, to support the mood of what the students are saying about the particular writers. (gradual move to independence)

5. Ask students to present an excerpt of the work of the writer with a selection of music from the same time period. It's important that the music be from the time period of the written piece, because as the music plays in the background, it conveys the mood of the work being read. (transfer and independence)

Literary Remix in Action

Diane begins this lesson by introducing her students to author Zora Neale Hurston. Diane did this in the form of a flashback by pretending to be at a reading where an unknown reader shared Hurston's 1928 essay *How It Feels to Be Colored Me* (2000). Thinking aloud, Diane pretends to have her thoughts interrupted by a flashback of growing up with her friend Zora Neale Hurston in Eatonvile, Florida, the first all-black town to be incorporated in the United States. Diane uses this format to develop Hurston's character, to introduce the technique of telling a story through a flashback because this was the technique Hurston used to tell the story in her 1937 novel *Their Eyes Were Watching God*, and to support a later discussion that will illustrate that Diane, by being white, easily could have felt marginalized in Eatonville. The think-aloud also shows the difficulties Hurston had with the concept of racism later in life due to the lack of such profiling in Eatonville. Here, Diane builds background knowledge and interest in the topic, which will be needed to support students' later independent work.

After her presentation, Diane invites her students to partner talk about the following topics: (a) their experiences with racism, (b) factors they think often constitute racist thoughts and actions, (c) how flashback is used in films they've seen, and (d) questions they have about Hurston. She asks the students to address all of these topics, because she wants to assess the range of the students' background knowledge with each of these four areas related to the lesson goals. As they chat, Diane asks them to take notes about the ideas they are sharing. She also takes notes as she moves among the students, listening in on their conversations, answering questions that do not derail their conversations, and posing additional questions to support and move their thinking across all of these areas. She is interested in assessing if they have addressed all of the identified areas. This knowledge will help her plan the next instructional steps to support the students in accomplishing the targeted goals. Listening in on her students offers an assessment of what they know about racism, flashback as a literary technique, and Hurston.

Next, in a conversational manner, the students share their experiences and insights and pose questions about Hurston, Eatonville, and the lack of racism in Eatonville. After this rich discussion, students are invited by Diane to explore text and Internet sources to gather background information to answer students' remaining questions about Hurston, her experiences with racial profiling, and whether flashback had been used in any of her writings. Each student is instructed to find five or more interesting pieces of information about each of these topics. As the students work, Diane again circulates among them to offer various types of support as needed and jots down a few notes about their performance.

For example, one student, Sarah, a young Muslim woman, continues to share all of her experiences with being profiled. Diane suggests that she begin journaling about these experiences and offers to respond to the journal entries. Happy with this opportunity, Sarah begins reviewing the works of Hurston. Another student, Robert, quickly lists five additional facts about Hurston. Diane encourages him to add enough detail so that if she hadn't known Hurston, she would be able to do so from his presentation of information. Josephine, who previously had read many of Hurston's works, becomes quite intrigued with the use of flashback as the literary technique in *Their Eyes Were Watching God* and relates this to how the technique had been used by Orsen Welles in the 1941 film *Citizen Kane*.

Once students collect the information about Hurston, Diane asks them to reorganize it to support their writing of paragraphs introducing her by sharing information on her background, beliefs, and accomplishments. She also asks the students to be prepared to present their paragraphs orally to the whole class as if the students were television commentators introducing a new celebrity. To prepare, the students practice via Photo Booth software to make these introductions, which include evaluative statements about why Hurston was an important figure worth knowing. Viewing and listening to themselves through Photo Booth provides an opportunity for the students to self-evaluate the content and delivery of their information. These written statements offer an example of what has been learned, synthesized, and shared in written presentation. Continuous performance assessment is a must when implementing a gradual release model of instruction.

Once students complete their introductions and presentation performances, they read Hurston's essay *How It Feels to Be Colored Me*, which can be located on the Internet. Diane asks the students to reflect on what Hurston was saying about life, people, and our country in the essay and to consider what life was like in the 1920s during the Harlem Renaissance, so they can contextualize Hurston's work historically.

After considering Hurston's message and their own personal feelings about what she was saying, students write imaginary dialogues between themselves and Hurston. In their dialogues, they include their own personal reactions to Hurston's essay and how they thought she would respond to their comments and questions. Students share their responses with partners, then search online for photos of Hurston. They use these and ones of themselves to create and share their dialogue through Comic Life software. In this exercise, students are encouraged to remix their existing and new literacies. Diane believes her students share more, because they enjoy creating a blend of imagery and conversation between themselves and Hurston, which simplified complex interpretations of her beliefs as well as the issues of the time period, by conveying this information in small chunks of dialogue.

The class next shifts focus to another famous writer of the same era, Langston Hughes. Similar to the background research they did on Hurston, students begin by investigating five or more interesting pieces of information on Hughes. In addition, to build more background on this author, they listen to a podcast of him telling about how he became interested in poetry. In a similar way, as they did with Hurston, students are asked to introduce Hughes by telling about his background, beliefs, and accomplishments. In addition, they are to determine from a comparison of the two authors' works if Hughes had the same beliefs about racism as did Hurston. The students are asked to support their assertions with examples or quotes from their research. Before sharing their introductions to Hughes, students select music that they believe will support the mood of what they are saying about him.

After students share their introductions to Langston Hughes, they read his poem "Harlem" (1951), which is also available online. Students write paragraphs that summarize the poem and explain why they feel it is significant. In addition, they discuss if (and why) they feel the poem is still relevant today. In their essays, students also make connections between Hughes's poem, Martin Luther King's famous "I Have a Dream" speech (1963), and Hurston's thinking. Students also include their own personal reactions to the messages of the themes brought forth by Hughes, King, and Hurston. Students then discuss their work with partner groups. As students share, Diane again listens in and chats, as would a member of the group; students have now moved to independence.

After sharing their reflective essays based on one of Hughes's poems, students select another of his poems to present to the class. As students orally interpret their selected poems, they also play music they've selected from the time period to support the mood of their poetry reading. During the sharing, two students with very different home discourse communities find that they have both selected "I, Too, Sing America" (1998), but have chosen different accompanying tunes. After listening to each other present, they ask if they can have some extended time to select a tune that they feel will represent both of them. They select "Introduction" by the Chicago Blues All Stars (1970, side 1 track 1). When the two students next jointly present the poem to the class, they follow their reading with a YouTube video, which they explain exemplifies their feelings (see Figure 3).

A final activity again invites the students to use Comic Life as well as photos of Langston Hughes and Zora Neale Hurston to create a conversation the students might have had with the two authors (see Figure 4). *Mule Bone* (Hughes & Hurston, 1930/1991) is a play that was jointly written by Hughes and Hurston but published only by Hurston; it is believed the tensions that arose while they worked on this play damaged their friendship. As students share their Comic Life examples in class, they talk about the importance of audience in selecting the appropriate discourse patterns for communicating their thoughts.

Figure 3. Langston Hughes Literary Remix

The poem below was read to the song "Introduction" by the Chicago Blues All Stars[a] and a YouTube™ video.

"I, Too, Sing America" by Langston Hughes (1926)[b]

I, too, sing America.

I am the darker brother.
They send me to eat in the kitchen
When company comes,
But I laugh,
And eat well,
And grow strong.

Tomorrow,
I'll be at the table
When company comes.
Nobody'll dare
Say to me,
"Eat in the kitchen,"
Then.

Besides,
They'll see how beautiful I am
And be ashamed—

I, too, am America.

Presented by Lajuana and Jennalisa (pseudonyms)

They followed their reading with this selection from YouTube: www.oprah.com/article/world/20090119_tows_americassong

---

[a]From Chicago Blues All Stars, 1970, "Introduction," on *American Folk Blues Festival '70* [Record], Germany: L+R Records, retrieved October 30, 2009, from mp3.rhapsody.com/album/american-folk-blues-festival-70--1989?artistId=art.41918. [b]From J.L. Hughes, 1998, I, Too, Sing America [Poem written 1926], in C. Clinton & S. Alcorn (Eds.), *I, Too, Sing America: Three Centuries of African American Poetry* (p. 9), New York: Houghton Mifflin.

Figure 4. A Student's Fabricated Conversation With Langston Hughes and Zora Neale Hurston Created With Comic Life Software

(continued)

Literary Remix Wrap-Up

Over the course of several weeks, students in Diane's class gain a historic perspective on racism by investigating the works of these two famous African American writers. Students develop key areas of literacy skills and competencies as they engage in critical analysis and conversation around their varied readings, writings, and discourse patterns. Additionally, they use research tools and skills to remix multimodal content and form new interpretations of texts.

Diane can use work samples and notes from the many class discussions as assessment data, giving her key insight into the abilities of her students to engage in complex literacy tasks. After completing the multimodal performances of Hughes's work, the class continues with their investigation of racism by expanding the focus to include other ethnic groups and examining the issue in the context of present-day society. Students speculate and explore the causes of racism and racial profiling as well as their own experiences with both. Finally, they propose potential solutions to the problem of racial profiling. After being introduced to the 1959 play *A Raisin in the Sun* by Lorraine Hansberry (1959/2004), the title of which comes from the opening line of Hughes's poem "Harlem," the students decide to present the play as a Readers Theatre performance as a culminating unit activity.

Similar to Ms. Friedman's lesson, Diane's instruction is an example of culturally responsive teaching that attempts to make instruction and the subsequent learning by the students reflective and responsive to their lives (Gay, 2002). This happens by taking the lead from students about their interests and strengths and then introducing instruction that the students find engaging. In these classrooms, the demarcation between teacher and students is replaced by a community of learners where the one who has the knowledge at the time becomes the one who takes the lead in the learning. This occurs often for teachers who are culturally responsive, because their students are much more knowledgeable than they are about technological possibilities. Coupled with all that teachers know about literacy learning, the result is a classroom without downtime for boredom—a classroom in which the social, cultural, language, and intellectual capital of all members of the learning community is enhanced as well as respected.

Using Remix to Expand Oral Discourse in the Classroom

As technological development changes the literacy practices and demands for people of the 21st century, it is vitally important that schools adapt how we teach language arts to stay relevant and provide the education our students need. This does not mean throwing out what we know about reading and writing curriculum and pedagogy. It does, however, call for new approaches and expanded definitions of language learning, comprehension, and literacy instruction. Oral discourses are ever changing and ever expanding and, given the interconnectedness of present society, diverse oral competencies are required from citizens. Now more than ever, we need to focus on ways to help students develop and expand oral discourses and always do so with a critical lens, so as to help students gain needed tools to filter and analyze the vast amounts of information now at their fingertips. In this chapter, we shared snippets of instruction offered as examples of ways we have addressed this current need through lessons that incorporate the remixing of content and strategies that help students gain critical independence in multimodal reading comprehension and language expression. We hope these examples will inspire many others, always with the goal of creating space for students to identify, analyze, celebrate, evaluate, and practice the presence of increasingly diverse oral discourses that touch and enrich all of our lives.

CHAPTER 4

Read It Well: Thinking Critically Across Multiple Texts

Surviving and thriving as a professional today demands two new approaches to the written word. First, it requires a new approach to orchestrating information, by skillfully choosing what to read and what to ignore. Second, it requires a new approach to integrating information, by reading faster and with greater comprehension.

Jimmy Calano, inspirational speaker

When observing your students, what are the exhibited behaviors that help you identify those who can read proficiently? Is it much more than just being able to word call, even when word calling is done very fluently? We believe reading well is exhibited by students who are able to use multiple processes automatically to create the meaning of a text actively. We use the word *create* because the act of reading or comprehending a text is an interactive process that occurs between the reader and the text (Afflerbach, Pearson, & Paris, 2008; Anderson & Pearson, 1984; Davis, 1944; Pressley, Johnson, Symons, McGoldrick, & Kurita, 1989; Vasquez, 2004). This creation happens as proficient readers automatically activate networks of existing knowledge, or schema, when they meet familiar topics or words in the text. A reader often begins with a purpose for their reading, such as for enjoyment, to complete homework assignments, to secure new information, or to solve a problem—the reasons are endless. Once the process begins, connections are made among the reader's existing schemas. So it is logical that the larger the reader's vocabulary and bases of knowledge and experience, the greater the possible range of comprehension will be.

While reading, proficient readers also employ the processes of reading that are traditionally referred to as "the act of reading." Involved behaviors during the act of reading include decoding typographic print messages, understanding that print works as symbols to represent language sounds (phonics), and deciphering the author's intended meanings of the text (comprehension). During reading, one also remembers and processes many pieces of information while maintaining focused attention.

After reading, proficient readers think about what they experienced while interacting with the text. Did they learn what was intended, and were their expectations met (Paris, Lipson, & Wixson, 1983; Pressley, 2000)? When proficient readers are unable to acquire meaning while interacting with a text, they figure out what went wrong and how to solve the problem. This ability to actively think about how you are thinking is called metacognition.

What Has Been Learned About Reading Recently?

Currently, the act of reading needs to be defined more broadly because of the multiple text types that continue to appear and also because of increased attention to the literacy skills that are needed to gain and share information via the new literacies of the Internet and ICTs. While still noting the importance of decoding and interpreting a variety of symbolic forms of meaning making, these are no longer limited to typographic print. Although few would argue against the importance for students to learn traditional or foundational reading skills, routines, and processes, educators now recognize multiple literacies that are vital for citizenry today. Therefore, in our current digitized world, to "read text well" conjures images quite different from, yet related to, our historical understandings of the same construct. Indeed, reading and teaching reading today involve a remix of existing and new research-based knowledge (Israel & Duffy, 2008; Ostenson, 2009).

Along with broadened concepts of what counts as text, and therefore expanded definitions of reading, is an emphasis on readers' processes of constructing meaning while engaging with texts (Coiro, 2003). When text is considered broadly, our understanding that meaning does not lie in the text itself but in the transaction between reader and text is reinforced. All texts are constructions and all texts are value laden: produced by people and bearing intentional and unintentional biases from the author. Likewise, readers do not approach texts as blank slates waiting to be filled by new information. Instead, readers bring prior knowledge and experiences to the task of deciphering meaning. They also bring their intentional and unintentional biases. With this understanding of reading as meaning construction, or negotiation, based on transactions between texts and readers situated in particular social, cultural, and historical contexts, comes a heightened importance for critical literacy.

Called to Action: The Need to Think Critically Across Multiple Texts

Critical literacy, interrogating underlying values, power dynamics, and assumptions of particular texts position readers as active meaning makers who have the power to read between the lines of texts, question hidden meanings based on oppressive social structures, and take action to help transform injustice. In essence, reading well is of central importance for participation in a democracy where we are daily asked to act and react in a variety of ways to varied situations.

For example, it is not uncommon to hear politicians urging listeners to perform their civic responsibilities as patriotic citizens by engaging in more consumer spending. After September 11, 2001, George Bush famously advised U.S. citizens to shop (Klein, 2002). Similar calls to jump-start the economy through shopping have been expressed in many periods of recession. The idea that spending money will stimulate the economy and therefore help the country thrive may seem reasonable given that a great deal of employment can be linked to consumer spending. However, proficient readers, or those who are critically literate, would interrogate texts, and in this case the link between shopping and patriotism would need to be unpacked. Rather than blind consumption, this unpacking would occur as a critical consumer-reader looked beneath the surface and asked analytical questions about who is truly benefiting, who is being shortchanged, whose voice is left out, and who is being heard. Reader-thinkers who are able to do this are considered to be critically literate, because they are able to go beyond the message conveyed by the author, as they interrogate the situation, and analyze the possible roles, beliefs, values, and actions of the people within the context (Alvermann et al., 1999). This invites a contrastive analysis of the points of view and actions of the authors and the situations that have been implied and constructed.

Was Critical Literacy Always the Goal of Literacy Education?

Years ago when students learned to read by reciting lines in one-room schoolhouses, a much more literal analysis may have been appropriate. Again using the topic of consumerism as a lens, we realize that it was not difficult, for example, to know where products came from. People largely made their own clothes and grew a great deal of their own food. In towns with general stores, people bought bulk items such as oats and grains from familiar shopkeepers who scooped only the amount requested from large storage bins.

Reading instruction shifted as small schoolhouses gave way to schools designed to serve greater segments of the population. These new schools were modeled after the factories that were springing up to mass-produce items for market. With the greater efficiency, both in production and in schooling, came a less familiar, perhaps even dehumanizing, feeling. To reassure consumers during this new industrial age, products' design responded to social uncertainty of the new and unfamiliar packaging. Instead of the shopkeeper scooping grains from a bin, a picture of a shopkeeper appeared on a factory-produced box of oatmeal (Klein, 2002). With industrialization, packaging containing "familiar" faces helped humanize production and make consumers feel comfortable with mass-produced products that would be unknown otherwise.

With globalization, it becomes harder and harder to trace the origins of the products we consume. As Annie Leonard (n.d.) points out, a simple plastic radio that you might buy in a big-box store for under $5 is not so simple when you consider the history of its fabrication. The radio is likely to contain metals from South Africa, petroleum from Iraq, and plastics made in China. All the parts probably were shipped to a factory in Mexico for assembly. From extraction to production, this radio has spanned the globe and affected lives of numerous people. In addition, this inexpensive radio has traveled numerous voyages via boat and truck before it arrives in the store for you to buy it. Let's not forget that it costs money to maintain the store and its employees who sell these radios.

How is it possible that one product with such a history can be sold so cheaply? What are the hidden costs of such a purchase? Who is really benefiting from the sale of such items? What part of the story is not being told? Answering these questions involves an analysis that critically literate thinkers engage in automatically. As educators in the 21st century, complete with Internet, personal computers, and globalization, we must provide instruction that supports students becoming educated citizens who can think critically about each situation in which they find themselves. In this consumer spending situation, answering the above questions helps readers realize what it means to be patriotic and what their civic responsibilities are.

Just as it did in previous time periods, reading instruction needs to change with the new demands faced by citizens. In an information age, critical literacy involving reading and writing in multiple modes is imperative. The following examples from Ms. Woollven and Robert Cheshire's 12th-grade English–social studies integrated classroom illustrate the notion that reading well in our present society involves remixing old and new literacies technologies in multiple and multimodal ways across the curriculum. The students in Ms. Woollven and Mr. Cheshire's class read their world by researching the histories of many of the products they use on a daily basis.

The lessons shared in the following pages are from a series of lessons designed to teach a number of skills highlighted by the IRA/NCTE English language arts standards (1996). In these lessons, Ms. Woollven and Mr. Cheshire aimed to teach their students to read and interpret multiple forms of texts, including print and nonprint, as well as conduct research to gather, synthesize, and analyze information from a variety of sources. At the end of the lessons, students should be able to communicate their findings and interpretations of their research in ways that are appropriate for different purposes and audiences.

Lesson Example 3: The Story of Stuff

In the book *No Logo: No Space, No Choice, No Jobs,* Klein (2002) documents a growing movement of people worldwide who question blind consumption. These people are especially concerned with the environmental and humanitarian issues related to the increasingly large multinational corporations responsible for the majority of products we consume daily. Similarly, Goleman's (2009) book *Ecological Intelligence: How Knowing the Hidden Impacts of What We Buy Can Change Everything* discusses the fact that sellers and producers know things that buyers generally do not. Through life cycle assessment and expanding our knowledge of the history of the things we buy, we can become more educated and selective consumers with the power to pressure companies to produce goods that are less harmful to the environment and less exploitative of workers.

The Story of Stuff Overview

The website *The Story of Stuff With Annie Leonard* (Leonard, n.d.) outlines what Leonard refers to as the "materials economy" by tracing products through the cycle from extraction to disposal (see Figure 5). She explains the danger of running a linear system on a finite planet: depletion of the earth's resources. She questions the role of government in helping big corporations perpetuate a system that drains resources and exploits human labor in the name of profit. Her argument points out the shortsightedness of a wasteful consumerist society that is based on quick profits and unequal distribution of wealth. Like Goleman (2009), Leonard posits that recycling is helpful but not enough. She offers suggestions of

Figure 5. The Structure of the Materials Economy

Extraction→ Production→ Distribution→ Consumption→ Disposal

Extraction: The mining of raw materials that are often nonrenewable and require a process that is harmful to the environment and people.

Production: Often characterized by exploitation of workers with no other options (e.g., many from areas decimated by extraction) and pollution from factories.

Distribution: The selling of "stuff" as quickly as possible with the goal of keeping costs down. Often store workers do not make good salaries and lack appropriate health care coverage.

Consumption: The heart of the materials economy. Products are often designed with limited lives to perpetuate the need of continual buying.

Disposal: Filling landfills with garbage at an alarming rate. Recycling helps but is not enough.

Note. Because the system is linear, it requires continued extraction. Since a great deal of the earth's resources are nonrenewable, we face the problem of their depletion. Adapted from A. Leonard, n.d., *The Story of Stuff With Annie Leonard*, retrieved May 10, 2009, from www.storyofstuff.com.

"another way" of doing things to address the problems, including reducing consumption and waste, making conscious efforts to patronize businesses that engage in green technologies and fair labor practices, and voicing opinions and educating others about the issues. Her website includes a movie about the materials economy, resources for further reading, and many other educational resources relating to the issues. Students can "read" the video as informational text, then explore the issues and claims made within. The following steps outline how you can do this:

1. To begin, show students Leonard's 20-minute video *The Story of Stuff* (found at storyofstuff.com/downloads.html) to learn about the concept of the materials economy. (building background knowledge)

2. Then in small groups, students select 15 facts presented in the movie and use the Internet to investigate the claims. Teachers identify the group compositions using a wide set of criteria such as friendships, strengths of students across all literacies, and work styles. (collaborative learning)

3. The small groups work to create an annotated bibliography to document their responses to the facts they investigated and the sources they drew on to arrive at their conclusions. (collaborative learning)

4. Finally, the groups present their findings to class. (independence)

The Story of Stuff in Action

The students in Ms. Woollven's and Mr. Cheshire's 12th-grade combined English–social studies class are accustomed to group work. Throughout the year, the students have engaged in a variety of project-based inquiry learning lessons designed to engage them in multimodal and hands-on learning. In earlier lessons, the teachers taught the students how to question a text to determine the veracity of the author's statements.

Both teachers are committed to teaching their students to become critical readers and engaged citizens who in their careers will probably be required to work with others near and far as the Web continues to support our global society. The teachers often incorporate Internet-based activities into their lessons, because they see the importance for young people learning to navigate such spaces with critical lenses. Prior lessons that would serve as the bases for this current project involved teaching the students to critically analyze information and Web resources.

Introduce the Task. For *The Story of Stuff* lesson, Ms. Woollven and Mr. Cheshire want students to consider how economic practices affect the environment and people. In the first part of this lesson, students critically view a short Internet movie, then investigate its claims. Here are the instructions the teachers provide to their students during this guided instruction phase of the lesson:

> Your assignment is to analyze the 20-minute movie created by Annie Leonard, *The Story of Stuff*. It is packed with data, statistics, and claims. Are they correct? Has she stretched the truth or downright misled her audience? Your challenge is to research at least 15 pieces of information that Ms. Leonard has included in her movie, including something from each of the first six sections (Introduction, Extraction, Production, Distribution, Consumption, and Disposal) to find out how accurate her movie really is. Each piece of information must be supported by at least three documented sources.
>
> Lastly, you should research one of the alternatives that Ms. Leonard says are currently being explored in the Another Way section of her movie. Explain what it is and whether your team thinks this method has a reasonable possibility for widespread public acceptance. You will present your findings to us in class.

Students Engage in Critical Analysis. As students watch the short movie, they take notes to record many facts laid out by Leonard. Students then work with their small group teams to select 15 facts, some from each section of the movie. Since it is filled with statistics, many that relate to environmental issues and are quite alarming, students have no trouble finding 15. The groups select many examples from the movie that relate to consumption of natural resources, issues of waste disposal, and other environmental issues. After selecting their items, student groups set out to prove or disprove the truth claims. Ms. Woollven and Mr. Cheshire move among the groups to offer various types of help as needed.

Even with students who are technologically savvy, doing research on the Internet can be a difficult task. Although there is a wealth of information available, it is well publicized that not all of the information is reliable. Before the Internet, research in classrooms was generally limited to the availability of books in the school and local libraries. Now the possibilities of student research are seemingly limitless. With a few clicks of a mouse, students can gain a wealth of information from multiple sources on practically any topic imaginable. With this opportunity come some new dilemmas primarily related to the credibility of sources. Although there are no easy answers to this question, there are a few measures that we address with students to help them sift through the vast, and often unfiltered, data they encounter during Internet-based research. Addressing the question of validity of sources with students provides a wonderful opportunity to initiate discussion about critical literacy. Such pedagogy focuses on information literacy and reflects the growing need for citizens to be able to evaluate and synthesize information from multiple sources.

For this assignment, students are challenged to investigate truth claims from a movie by filtering through questionable information sources. Just as Ms. Woollven and Mr. Cheshire point out in their instructions, truth is often stretched, and information can be misleading. We like to emphasize this, because it is the challenge and the joy of reading comprehension with any type of text. Since the Internet provides some novel and unique challenges, we offer some specific guidance for students when using the Web for research purposes in Table 5. Other resources you may wish to investigate include

- R. Harris, June 15, 2007, *Evaluating Internet Research Resources*, retrieved October 30, 2009, from www.virtualsalt.com/evalu8it.htm

- W. Howe, April 2001, *Evaluating Quality*, retrieved October 30, 2009, from www.walthowe.com/navnet/quality.html

- D.J. Leu et al., 2007, What Is New About the New Literacies of Online Reading Comprehension? in L.S. Rush, A.J. Eakle, & A. Berger (Eds.), *Secondary School Literacy: What Research Reveals for Classroom Practice* (pp. 37–68), Urbana, IL: National Council of Teachers of English.

Table 5. Internet Research Guidelines

- Always check the sources of information. Virtually anyone can create a webpage and claim expertise on a topic. Students should check the About or Info sections of the websites for potential biases or hidden agendas of the authors. The Links To feature can also be used to learn about who links to the particular site, which can also help in judgments of credibility.

- Try to cross-check information by using multiple sources. More sites with similar information increases the likelihood that the information is reliable.

- If possible, check the date the page was last updated. The more recent the posting, the probability of more up-to-date information increases.

- Popularity does not always mean credibility. The first hits for most search engines will include the sites with the most links. Although this can indicate validity, it is not always the case. Further discussion on this topic with the class is highly useful.

- Cite sources of information. Students need to know that both direct quotes and paraphrasing of information require citation, which strengthens the credibility of the work.

Note. Adapted from C. Shamburg, 2008, *English Language Arts Units for Grades 9–12*, Eugene, OR: International Society for Technology in Education.

After selecting different topics from the video, students conducted Internet research and created annotated bibliographies that included information sources not connected to Leonard's website. Although the task proved challenging, students were able to find a variety of Internet sources relating to the many topics addressed in the video. Once complete, the students shared their findings from their bibliographies with the rest of the class. In the class discussion, the group agreed that Leonard's claims seemed accurate, although perhaps in some cases exaggerated. One savvy student directed the class's attention back to the website where she found a transcript of the video with footnotes containing bibliographic information about the information sources that Leonard used to make her truth claims.

Lesson Example 4: The Story of *Our* Stuff

Building on the concepts learned in the lesson related to Annie Leonard's (n.d.) video *The Story of Stuff*, this next lesson asks students to take the next step in becoming critically literate consumers by investigating and reflecting on their personal connections to the information. Called The Story of *Our* Stuff, the lesson engages students in original research with the goal of students exploring the life cycles of products that are familiar to them and used by them.

The Story of Our Stuff Overview

Because the corporations that profit from the production and distribution of consumer goods do not necessarily wish for consumers to be fully knowledgeable about the origins and implications of the products they use, it can be difficult to uncover a great deal of specific information about products' actual histories. Even when contacting companies, roadblocks such as proprietary secrets get in the way of a comprehensive uncovering of a product's life cycle. Therefore, in this lesson, students learn not only about specific products but also about the process of investigation. One of the big learning points here is that some information is well guarded. The following are steps to take when guiding students through a lesson on researching the histories of commonly used products:

1. Begin with students in small groups selecting a product that they use on a daily basis. (getting started)

2. Ask groups to research the life cycle of the product. The research tactics can include Internet searches, e-mails and phone calls to companies and consumer organizations, and library research. (collaborative learning)

3. When finished, ask groups to present their findings in a research paper. (collaborative learning)

4. Groups use research to create the "story" of their product in a multimodal format, such as a comic strip or short movie. (collaborative learning)

5. Ask students to present their projects to others in class during their gallery walk, which is described later in the chapter. (collaborative learning)

The Story of Our Stuff in Action

After investigating and presenting their findings of facts from the movie *The Story of Stuff*, the students turn their research lenses on their own consumption habits. The following are instructions that initiate the lesson for the 12th graders to begin exploring the life cycles of common products:

> Your teachers challenge you to personalize the process that Ms. Leonard described in her movie *The Story of Stuff*. We want you to research an item you use on a frequent basis to discover how that item fits into the materials economy process of extraction, production, distribution, consumption, and disposal. What materials were used to make the item? What happened before it came into your possession? Once your research is complete, you

will personify your item to create an interesting yet informative portrayal of your findings—"The Adventures of Ollie the Alarm Clock," for example.

Step 1: After conducting extensive research on an approved item of your choice, you will each write a research report explaining your findings.

Step 2: Teams will create a movie or a comic book to bring only one of your team's chosen items to life.

It's important to note that prior projects involved similar tasks, so the teachers knew the students would be able to perform these tasks. This is how the teachers used collaborative learning and lesson scaffolding to help ensure students' understanding and success.

In small groups, students brainstorm and debate common products that they would like to investigate. Students with broad interests and experiences propose items such as beauty products, office supplies, popular electronic devices, and household goods. Once the groups narrow their ideas, they sign up with the teachers to make sure that there is variety and that no two groups are exploring the same item. Some examples of group selections include ping-pong paddles, computer printers, energy bars, socks, and hair weave. To get as specific as possible, groups select particular brands of the products they choose.

Over the course of a couple of weeks, students spend time using the Internet to research, contact companies via e-mail, and learn as much as possible about their selected items. For each stage in the life cycle of their products, students are guided by teacher-provided questions that need to be addressed (see Table 6). The questions are categorized according to the different phases of the life cycle of a product. The questions were designed to encourage critical reading and thinking and include questions relating to environmental and human impact in the various stages of the life cycle. For example, when researching extraction, students are not simply asked to list the materials used to make the product and where they came from. The guiding questions relating to extraction also direct students' attention to the effects on people who are involved in the process and people who live near the areas the raw materials are mined from. Similarly, guiding questions for other phases of the products' life cycles push students to think about human and environmental effects that can be considered the subtext of each product and its relation to consumers.

As students gather information, they create websites for their group members to compile and organize what they find. Each group creates a page using Google Groups, so each member can access the information from within or outside of school when they have use of a computer with

Table 6. Questions to Guide Students' Product Research

Part 1: Extraction
- Describe all of the materials used to make the item.
- From what natural resources did these materials come?
- Describe where and how each resource was extracted from the earth. What effect does the extraction have on the people involved in the extraction? What about the people who live near the extraction location?

Part 2: Production
- Describe where the item is assembled (i.e., geographical location and type of factory, mill, sweatshop, etc.).
- Describe how the materials are assembled to create the item.
- What, if any, chemicals are used in the production process?
- What are the working conditions for the people involved in the production of the item?
- What impact does the production of the item have on the environment?

Part 3: Distribution
- How does the item get from its place of production to a store?
- How does the transport of the item affect the environment?

Part 4: Consumption
- How is the item advertised?
- Describe an advertisement used to sell the item.
- What types of stores is the item typically sold in?
- What are the typical wages and working conditions of the workers of those stores?
- What is the average life span of your item?

Part 5: Disposal
- What are some typical reasons that the item would be disposed of?
- What are all the possible methods of disposing your item?
- How does the disposal of the item affect the environment?

Internet access. Students compile data on the various stages of the life cycle of their products and store their references in this shared space. Similar to a wiki, a Google Group is a free, online space for individuals to share information. A group is created by an individual, who then can act as the group manager or invite another user to do so. The manager, a classmate and fellow group member, can invite other people to join the group. The groups share Web space where they can share and store information, have online discussions or discuss via e-mail, and create webpages inside the group. The manager posts messages to inform the other group members on how to post research and remind them to keep backup copies always in case of technology problems. Sharing and backing up information are two authentic issues in this era of computer-based literacy. For more information on how to create and maintain a Google Group, visit groups.google.com.

Digging Deeper. In this lesson, students have to transfer their knowledge bases to novel situations and remix their literacies while doing so. As their research progresses, the students find that Leonard's notion of a materials economy was not so easy to uncover. First, many products contain a wide array of parts that are composed of quite a variety of different materials from different regions of the world. Second, many companies are not forthcoming about releasing information about their products' life cycles. Although most products contain some kind of labeling about where they were manufactured, not much is divulged about where the materials come from or how workers are treated in production factories. Students contact companies via e-mail and a few even try telephoning, but most never receive any response from their companies. The few students who successfully get through learn that companies generally do not share such information, because they do not want to compromise their proprietary secrets. Often when students are able to gather general information about the contents of a product or the location of production, they can access information published independently that relates to environmental and working conditions in those regions. Although not necessarily specific to the students' chosen products, the information can be applied speculatively to them.

For example, one group chooses Hanes socks for their research. While investigating extraction, the group learns that a great deal of cotton used in clothing such as socks is grown in the Republic of Uzbekistan. Philip, one group member, explains how this finding triggers further exploration:

> "I had never heard of Uzbekistan, and I wasn't sure if it really existed. So I looked it up on Google Maps. I always look stuff up to check my sources when I am doing research, because you never know, it could be like a hoax."

Philip's words demonstrate an understanding of cross-checking information sources to increase reliability of final information chosen. He further explains that while looking up agriculture in Uzbekistan, he learned that it is the second-biggest producer of cotton in the world and that approximately one third of the people in that country are involved in the industry. In addition, the country has been implicated in widespread use of child labor for cotton production. Similarly, he found that the socks his group was studying are made in China. Again he was unable to find specific information about the factories in China that made this particular brand of socks, but he read a great deal of information regarding atrocious working conditions for factory workers in that part of the world. He tried to learn specifics about the company and their production by looking at their website and sending them an e-mail; however, he was unable to get any useful information from them. He speculates that companies "don't want us to know about how the socks are made or where they are made, because we would be appalled and probably wouldn't buy them."

Although new technology makes way for new literacies that are important to address in school, traditional forms of written communication are still necessary. Ms. Woollven and Mr. Cheshire understand this and have included a traditional-style research report in the design of the larger research project. After students complete their investigations of the life cycles of their selected products, they write reports detailing what they learned. Since this style of report was something that students had done on numerous occasions throughout the year, the teachers did not spend time giving instruction on the format for the reports. Students know that their reports need to include a cover page with a title, their names, the date, the item researched, and the company that produces the product. The body of the report needs to be organized well with an introduction, sections addressing each phase of the life cycle and answering each of the guiding questions, and a conclusion that includes a reflection on the research process. Finally, as was the case in other research projects, students are required to create a works cited page using MLA style for their references.

Critical Analysis Involves Finding More Than Is Expected. During the process of researching and reflecting on common products, many students are surprised by information that is often kept beneath the surface. One group chooses to research Converse All Stars, a popular brand of sneakers. They report that they were shocked to learn that the company had been bought out by Nike. Since this change in management, the production moved from factories in the United States to factories in China and Vietnam. Like the group studying socks, they found no specific information from the company that discussed working conditions for people who make the shoes. However, they did find a good amount of information connecting Nike and poor labor conditions for workers in Asia.

In their research report, the group highlights that Nike has not publicized the fact that they own Converse. Noting the popularity of Converse with hipster kids, the student group speculates that Nike wants to keep the information private to avoid losing this market. They conclude their paper by stating, "While Converse may have once been the staple of the American athletic scene and then progressed into a subculture necessity, they have in recent years been bought out and in our opinion corrupted." With this final reflective statement, the group demonstrates a historical understanding of the company's connection to U.S. culture and a critical analysis of hidden meanings of the text of the shoe industry and the larger materials economy. Their critical analysis of these Converse shoes is an excellent example of reading well using multiple sources and multiple text types.

Finally, student groups use their research papers to recreate the data regarding the life cycle of their products in a way that "brings to life" the stories of the items. Students are instructed to make a comic book or a short movie documenting the life history of their group's product. Already familiar with programs such as Comic Life, iMovie, and Movie Maker, students do not require instruction in technical aspects of the activity. Students find creative ways to tell the stories of their products, sometimes creating fictional autobiographies from the perspective of the products (see Figure 6). Other groups approach the task by showing their own learning about the products' life cycles through mock conversations between friends. Many other examples of comics and movies depict the "lives" of an array of products from energy bars to computer printers.

Figure 6. An Example of a Fictional Autobiography of a Product: The Story of an Aluminum Can (First Page)

Figure 7. An Example of a Presentation: The Story of a Computer Printer

As the culmination task of their research on life cycles of their own "stuff," student groups do a gallery walk. Groups take turns presenting and observing each other's presentations as they rotate through the classroom learning about the many different products that have been researched. As students present, their peers take notes and ask questions relating to the presentations (see Figure 7 for a presentation scene). The next segment of this unit of study illustrates how these teachers provide space for their students to move from critical reading to being critically literate as they make their voices heard in a way that might have an impact on making a better world for a larger populace.

Lesson Example 5: The Bubble Project: Talking Back to the Materials Economy

When studying the materials economy, especially in terms of the consumption stage being the heart of the system, students learn that educating one's self and others about environmental and human impacts of consumption is one way to try to improve conditions in the world. Through their research experiences, students corroborated Leonard's claims that corporations are not generally interested in transparency and would prefer for consumers not to think about the origins, histories, and impacts of

Table 7. Culture Jamming Resources

- Adbusters (www.adbusters.org): Dedicated to media literacy and culture jamming, this website contains many examples of spoof ads and other critiques on mass marketing and blind consumption.
- Billboard Liberation Front (www.billboardliberation.com): This site has many examples of culture jamming that specifically targets billboard advertising.
- The Bubble Project (www.thebubbleproject.com): This site gives background information and shows examples of bubbles that have been created to provide ordinary people with a means to speak back to mass media and advertising.
- FreewayBlogger (www.freewayblogger.com): This site shows many examples from activists who have posted signs on freeways voicing cultural criticism on a variety of topics.

Note. These websites, and many others that can be found via simple Internet searches or by looking at the links from these sites, show some examples of anticorporate activism that is occurring in many areas. For a more detailed account of this movement worldwide, we highly recommend reading N. Klein, 2002, *No Logo: No Space, No Choice, No Jobs* (2nd ed.), New York: Picador.

the products they use. In addition, to encourage more consumption, huge amounts of resources are dedicated to advertising to convince people that they need more stuff. One hope for change is to become educated and to educate others about issues, so people can collectively act to correct situations deemed problematic. This is the hallmark of critical literacy and participatory democracy.

The Bubble Project is one example of anticorporate activism designed to "talk back" to the corporations in regards to the incursions of ads on our daily lives. Many examples of culture jamming can be found worldwide and much has been written about this topic (see Table 7). Created by guerrilla artist Ji Lee, The Bubble Project gives ordinary people an opportunity to speak back to ads. By simply placing blank speech bubbles on advertisements in public spaces, Lee opens space for people to write dialogue and commentary about the ads. Although this is considered vandalism and is illegal, we have adapted the general idea for pedagogical purposes. Please note that many of the images on The Bubble Project's website contain adult content and language that may be inappropriate for school contexts; we highly recommend teachers first screen this site and select appropriate images to share with the class.

The Bubble Project Overview

Our version of The Bubble Project creates space in the classroom for students to dialogue about consumption and particularly the values put forth in mass media advertising. By placing speech bubbles with commentary on magazine ads, students voice their own ideas, interpretations, and critiques of the underlying messages found in the ads. Students use their critical literacy lenses to read and unpack hidden assumptions found in mass media, then remix the images to turn them on themselves to create new meanings, often as countertexts. The following steps provide an overview of a lesson that guides students in the critical reading of mass media:

1. First, ask students to do a quick-write on advertising by addressing issues like purpose, voice, and persuasion. (activating background)

2. Share a presentation of examples of culture jamming found on the Internet and invite group discussion about culture jamming and anticonsumerist activism. (guided discussion)

3. Finally, have students create their own examples of bubbles to talk back to advertisers and consumerism. (independence)

The Bubble Project in Action

Ms. Woollven wants her 12th graders to think about the large-scale incursion of advertising on all of our lives and consider how this bombardment plays a role in influencing our consumption habits as well as more broadly affecting our values. Her goal for this lesson is to have students unpack the values promulgated in mainstream media in general and specifically in advertising. In addition, she wants her students to consider ways to share critical viewpoints that can counter hegemonic messages that are often racist, sexist, oppressive, and unfair.

To activate background knowledge, Ms. Woollven engages students in a quick-write to activate and evaluate background knowledge. To quick-write, students are given a prompt and asked to write nonstop for a short period of time, usually two to five minutes. The writing is not to be turned in, but rather serves as a way to get thoughts flowing to initiate discussion on a certain topic. Quick-writing also gives the teacher insight about students' existing knowledge bases. For this quick-write, Ms. Woollven asks students to generate a list of all of the advertisements they can think of and where they find them. After making a list, students are asked to consider whose voice is heard in the advertisements and who is not heard.

Students engage in a lively discussion about ads on billboards, television, radio, the Internet, clothing, and many other places. They demonstrate the ability to be critical of false claims of advertising while understanding the impetus for companies to put forth persuasive arguments. The students generally do not fall into probusiness or anticorporate camps. Instead, they seem to hold balanced views that include critique and admiration for ads and the companies responsible for them.

Ms. Woollven then shares examples of anticorporate counter ads that were made by culture jammers. She selects a variety of examples she found on the websites of The Bubble Project and Adbusters. The examples from Adbusters are similar to those of The Bubble Project in that they serve as countertexts disrupting messages of mainstream ads. However, the Adbusters' examples are different, because rather than adding speech bubbles for anonymous citizens to talk back, Adbusters creates spoof ads by remixing images digitally (Lankshear & Knobel, 2006). While viewing a variety of examples of culture jamming of ads involving popular cigarettes, fast-food chains, beauty products, and fashion, students discuss probable motivations of the authors who created the counter ads.

Next, students are asked to create their own spoof ads, or counter ads, by selecting advertisements or other images from mass media and remixing them with personal commentary. Students read the status quo messages of the media and produce new texts by incorporating speech and thought bubbles that disrupt aspects of the originals. The students comment on many themes, including typical depictions of beauty, unrealistic expectations for body types, and unstated health risks of certain types of foods and drinks (see Figure 8). The student work is posted

Figure 8. An Example of Student Bubbling

in the school hallway for public observation. In this lesson, Ms. Woollven's students critically read advertisements and other popular media and rewrite them to bring critical subtext to the fore. The ads they create are intended to enlighten the consumer knowledge bases of their peers, so that the next time they are called upon to spend, they will hopefully understand how their actions positively and negatively affect economies and people worldwide.

Using Remix to Promote Critical Reading of Multiple Text Sources

In the lessons highlighted in this chapter, students learn about critical analysis, which is vital for citizenry in a healthy democracy. Through expanded notions of text and engagement with multimodal materials, reading comprehension instruction adapts to connect traditional reading skills with newer skills associated with the changing face of information in the 21st century. Through various activities, students deconstruct and interrogate text related to consumption and consumerism. By analyzing and synthesizing information from varied sources and constructing new meanings through creation of multiple and multimodal texts, students remix materials in critical ways to arrive at new understandings of familiar texts. We believe that it is our role as educators to ensure that this critical analysis becomes as automatic to proficient readers as is reading fluently. In a sense, we believe this critical analysis becomes the 21st century's duality of automaticity within the reading process.

How Can These Lessons Be Adapted to Any Context?

The teachers in these lessons use a model that can be applied to any context in any of the following ways:

1. Engage students' literacy learning through an expanded notion of text. In the lesson examples, we share multiple modes of communication, such as those represented through websites and shown in the figures, which are counted as text and used for authentic "reading" and "writing." As in the cases highlighted in this chapter, students can use websites and search engines to research and analyze information that comes in printed text,

pictures, and video, then respond to the readings using multiple modes of meaning making (e.g., text, photos, video, combination).

2. Discuss and illustrate for students that all texts are social constructions. This means that meaning is situated in social, cultural, and historical contexts and is inherently value laden. Therefore, students should always be encouraged to interrogate texts for meanings that often remain beneath the surface.

3. Ensure that students have strong background knowledge about the topic being investigated. Through discussions and lesson examples 4 and 5, students realize the need to build such background knowledge. Multiple and varied sources of information are important for building comprehensive and nuanced understandings of topics. Through these discussions, students should be encouraged to reflect on their own beliefs and their underlying constructs. Students should soon recognize that how they read a text depends on how they read the world (Freire & Macedo, 1987).

4. Model for and support students as they learn to identify and question the author's premise. Texts cannot be taken at face value, and readers should always consider who created the text, for whom, and why.

5. Investigate and discuss the author's premise. Cross-checking the truth claims of the premises with contrastive points of view supports critical analysis.

6. Model how to analyze the subtext, or hidden values, present in the text. This involves considering how power dynamics play out in the given text. Students ask questions such as, Whose voice is privileged? Whose voice is absent or silenced? Why is the text privileging some experiences or realities over others?

7. Invite students to identify their roles in the situation. By reflecting on their connection to the questions being raised in the critical readings of the texts, students can situate themselves and their understandings within the sociohistoric moment and in relation to the text.

8. Encourage students to think about how to take action on any unjust situations or issues that were highlighted in analysis.

9. Discuss how every action can result in positive and negative consequences. Discuss the importance of thinking about this before acting.

10. Communicate new knowledge to extended audiences through various means. Rather than a school-based assignment that never goes beyond the walls of the classroom, with this sort of lesson, it is important to consider ways that students can share their learning with other classrooms, family members, friends, and others in the community.

CHAPTER 5

Write It Well: Focusing on Sharing Thoughts Through Writing

You have to write a million words before you find your voice as a writer.

Henry Miller

Think about what you've been doing for the last couple of days. What have you written? If you made a list, I bet it would include messages sent via phone texts, Twitter, Facebook, MySpace, and e-mail, to name a few. These are surely different from what might have been on your list of ways that you communicate through writing five years ago. Writing today is an integral part of one's daily social life as well as an integral part of the English language arts curriculum. As you reflect on your writing activities, it's obvious that writing is inherently tied to reading, and the two are considered reciprocal, or shared, processes, since one's writing activities involve reading, and reading activities often involve writing. Therefore, when teaching, it is difficult to separate reading and writing into two distinct areas. In this chapter, we highlight the process of writing as the focus of literacy lessons, illustrating how to expand traditional notions of both good writing and reading to include an array of new literacies practices. It is our belief that writing well in 21st-century terms means remixing old and new styles and skills for authentic communicative purposes.

What Does Traditional Writing Look Like in a Classroom?

Traditionally, writing instruction has centered on developing students' skills in constructing meaning through alphabetic print. Such practice has primarily focused on helping students learn the codes and structures of standard language text production. Decontextualized skills-based instruction that stresses drills of isolated grammar points have largely given way to more process-oriented approaches that imbed grammar and other stylistic lessons within more authentic writing tasks that are conducted and often initiated by students.

Process writing, often in the form of a writers' workshop, models for students how to move from idea conception to production of a written piece that may appear in many genre forms. A writers' workshop is also based on a gradual release model of instruction. With the goal of having students produce a wide array of pieces, teachers may be found modeling any of the recursive writing processes, including prewriting, drafting, revising, editing, and publishing. Students are supported as they learn how to develop thoughts from their inception as ideas to polished pieces ready for sharing with others (Brown & Campione, 1981; Fisher & Frey, 2003; Pearson & Gallagher, 1983).

As teachers and students work together within a writers' workshop format, it becomes quite clear that the process of writing any piece does not follow a clear linear sequence. Writing instruction cannot flow neatly in a step-by-step fashion from prewriting through to publication. Instead, teachers of writing help students understand the dynamic nature of the writing process. Through engaging in writing tasks deemed authentic by the writer, students participating in the workshop approach learn that the various stages in the process are not so much clearly defined steps as much as they are symbolic categories used to help writers develop their pieces.

Expanding Definitions of Writing

The invention of the Gutenberg press is considered by many to be one of the greatest human inventions. Certainly, in terms of literacy development, it ranks close to the top. Before movable type, the ability to read and write was largely the domain of society's ruling elite. The prohibitive cost of recreating texts, which had to be done painstakingly by hand, meant that the purchase of a single book would be inconceivable for anyone but the extremely rich. The advent of the printing press allowed books and other printed materials to filter to larger segments of the population, which led to increased literacy rates among common people.

Even with technology that brought literacy possibilities to a broader range of people, reading and writing were skills that were kept from disenfranchised segments of the world's populations. Often, the ruling elite forbade literacy or made schooling inaccessible for the poor in society. Literacy was seen as potentially dangerous, because it might lead people to question their living conditions. Should people be able to express thoughts in print and therefore to a larger audience not in their immediate presence, they potentially could express discord with certain oppressive social structures. There are countless examples throughout our global history that illustrate the power of the written word for liberation of oppressed peoples and how the literacy issue was contested and tightly controlled by the powerful.

New developments such as the Internet and digital technology are potentially as revolutionary as the development of the printing press. Today, publishing information is accessible to anyone anywhere who has access to the Internet. This means a small group of indigenous people who have been marginalized for centuries in a remote mountainous region of southern Mexico can gain a world audience to express their grievances with an authoritarian regime. Or the fallout after a disputed election in Iran can be broadcast by protesters in the street via cell phones to people all over the world. Or children in the United States can become virtual pen pals with children in South Africa by interacting through e-mail and Skype. Or a person in Hong Kong can read a blog written by a teenager in a small town in Canada. Or within seconds, the world learned that Michael Jackson had died. These and many more examples demonstrate how new digital technologies allow regular people to share thoughts, ideas, experiences, and meanings with others across the globe. Such expanded possibilities for publication created by the technology lead to a flattening of the traditionally hierarchical world of publishing, which serves as the gatekeeper for what print is deemed worthy of distribution.

When we consider the text that comprises the variety of sources we commonly access on the Internet, we see that writing no longer can be thought of as strictly typographic print. Along with an abundance of alphabetic print text are videos, digital still pictures, audio podcasts, and many other types of text, some of which combine visual and auditory modes of expression. In each case, authors are expressing meaning to audiences ("readers") through these multiple modes. As writing teachers, we need to push ourselves, and our students, to explore various modes of expression in the classroom.

Critical Literacy and Critical Text Production

Brazilian educator Paulo Freire famously described the process of becoming truly literate as reading the word and reading the world (Freire, 1970), referring to the idea that literacy can be a tool for human liberation. When students learn to read, broaden their understandings of the world and themselves, and begin to ask questions about their experiences, it can start a cycle of questioning and reflection that he called critical consciousness. In Freire's model, engagements with the written word and reflections on their knowledge of the world help students begin to take proactive stances for the betterment of humanity.

Freire's view of literacy is foundational for those who advocate a sociocultural view of writing. Such a view opens up writing as cultural practice in which beginners apprentice through interactions with texts and experts with authentic purpose (Morrell, 2008). As students read, analyze, and reflect upon various texts, they learn to critique often oppressive and unfair discourses that promote mainstream ideologies.

In classrooms that subscribe to a sociocultural view of literacy, student writing becomes what Morrell (2008) calls "critical textual production" (p. 115), or what Comber and Nixon (2005) call "counter narratives" (p. 129). In such instances, students begin with their own experiences and with real-world problems to develop texts that focus on social justice. Students' counter narratives are designed to name oppression and injustice, critique existing texts that promote status quo, and present other possibilities for more just futures. Morrell (2008) exemplifies a sociocultural view of writing instruction, stating,

> I can think of no better purpose for curricula that include critical writing than to take up the charge of developing writers as engaged citizens and transformative intellectuals who see writing as a tool, if not the tool, of social change. (p. 134)

By viewing writing as *the* tool of social change, teachers communicate to students the power of words for real-life consequences. Therefore, writing well becomes something that, in addition to leading to good grades in school, can also initiate social transformation and human liberation. When students engage in class-based writing that challenges oppressive status quo with the goal of transformation, they learn that their voice can be powerful and make a difference. Such agency is the hallmark of a truly democratic society.

Instruction That Expands the Concept of Authentic Text

This chapter highlights examples of writing in a classroom that promotes a sociocultural view of literacy. Students engage with multiple texts and use multiple modes for critical textual production. Starting with the analysis of mentor texts and reflecting on lived experiences, students explore writing as an act of naming injustices and then seeking solutions to the social problems. Students use both traditional academic modes of expression as well as other forms such as hip-hop poetry and digital storytelling to express their views and inform others.

It is of central importance that teachers provide a balance of traditional academic literacy and the new literacies that are so prevalent in the world today. Writing in standard language is still the currency for social mobility in most mainstream contexts. As teachers, we must continue to develop our students' abilities to write using the grammar, punctuation, form, and style of traditional writing instruction. At the same time, we can make space for students to develop new literacies skills for expression in a variety of modes. In fact, we believe that these two types of literacies are complementary and necessary for success in today's increasingly digitized world. The lessons highlighted in this chapter reflect this belief and provide students with opportunities for multimodal writing of counter narratives with authentic purposes and intentions of social transformation.

Teachers Alina Adonyi and Jennifer Woollven designed the following lessons when they taught together in a middle school. Ms. Woollven recently moved to the high school level, where she teaches language arts and adapted the unit for 11th and 12th graders. The classroom examples depicted in the following lessons come from her high school classroom. These lessons address the following skills outlined by IRA/NCTE (1996) standards:

- Students address a variety of audiences for a variety of purposes using multiple forms of communication, including print and nonprint texts.

- Students apply their knowledge of language and how it works (e.g., structure, conventions) in the creation and critique of multiple forms of text.

- Students pose problems, generate questions and ideas, and conduct research, then communicate their findings through multiple and multimodal texts with consideration for what is appropriate for their purpose and audience.

- Students can use a variety of technological and information resources (e.g., libraries, databases, computer networks, videos) to gather and synthesize information and create and communicate knowledge.

Lesson Example 6: Documentary Poetry

Throughout history, poetry has been considered by many cultures as a way for humans to examine, reflect on, and even transcend their worldly conditions. From the Greek philosophers to present-day hip-hop artists, poetry has served as a vehicle to relate not only what has happened but also what is possible (Morrell, 2008). Although this is not true of all poetry, many poets have used this artistic form of text production to document and make public the stories of people and movements often overlooked or ignored by mass media or mainstream history. Poetry that uses journalistic style and tools to provide testimonials of people who are struggling to survive is sometimes referred to as documentary poetry. Describing the documentary style of Nicaraguan poet Ernesto Cardenal, Pring-Mill (1980) likened the technique to that of film. He explains that Cardenal uses an almost photographic imagery with his words, and by pointing the lens in certain ways, it helps us mediate reality by both corroborating and debunking our impressions of the world around us.

Documentary poetry refers to poetry that informs and is informed by real-world events. This form uses poetry as testimony to document unjust social issues, especially relating to the stories of people whose voices often go unheard in mainstream news and history sources. Furthermore, this poetry advocates for social issues and calls others to action. Metres (2009) refers to these poets as journalists, documentarians, historians, and agitators. Poets who use their voices to foreground the voices and experiences of oppressed others create these counter narratives, or documentary poems, because they view poetry as having power to make change in real life outside of the poem itself. For documentary poets, "poetry is not a museum-object to be observed from afar, but a dynamic medium that informs and is informed by the history of the movement" (Metres, 2009, para. 3). Many songwriters can be viewed as poets as well, and we include the work of songwriters alongside poets for the purposes of our lessons on documentary poetry. There are considerable examples of poets who use documentary style, some who are quite well known and others who are less known, such as June Jordan, Walt Whitman, Pablo Neruda, Nikki Giovanni, Ernesto Cardenal, Allen Ginsberg, Bob Dylan, Martín Espada, Mos Def, and Lauryn Hill. In this chapter, we provide the names of some poets and poems that we believe exemplify this style of writing.

Documentary Poetry Overview

Students can learn about the power of words in lessons that guide them through analysis and production of texts. The following steps provide an overview of a lesson that focuses on documentary poetry:

1. Teacher and students read and discuss an example of documentary poetry that serves as a mentor text. The teacher takes the lead in the discussion. (modeling)

2. Students engage in minilessons modeled by the teacher about poetic devices used in documentary poetry. (guided practice)

3. With the teacher still modeling, students discuss and journal about social justice issues that are relevant to them and their lives. (guided practice)

4. Students then select important issues and write poems using forms and devices they learned from the mentor texts. (collaborative learning)

5. The students create digital poetry using computers to record audio and set their poems to images. (independence)

6. Finally, students share and discuss their work. (collaborative learning)

Documentary Poetry Lesson in Action

Like many high school students around the world, the young people in Ms. Woollven's 12th-grade language arts class enjoy listening to hip-hop music. Recognizing the great potential of tapping into the interests of her students while highlighting an important area of the curriculum, she decided to introduce the class to documentary poetry through an exploration of some critical hip-hop (Morrell & Duncan-Andrade, 2002). Having just listened to a friend perform an original spoken word poem, she decided that using her friend's poem as a mentor text would be a great entry point for the lesson. Ms. Woollven began with a mentor text written by this local artist, then introduced a series of other classic and contemporary poems. If you wish to replicate this lesson or create similar lessons based on documentary-style poetry, you can adapt Ms. Woollven's lesson to your own context. (See Table 8 for a sample list of poems and songs that employ documentary style to address social issues in their work.)

To begin, Ms. Woollven poses the following guiding question to the class: How can poetry function as a vehicle for social change? The 12th graders consider this question as they read, discuss, and reflect on the poem "Why I Write" by Tim Swain (n.d.), who lives in a town near the school and is a member of a group called Hip Hop Congress. With this group, he has performed this poem and others at area schools and organizations. "Why I Write" uses a multivoiced style to convey themes of diversity, responsibility, tolerance, and identity.

Table 8. Some Notable Documentary Poems and Songs, and Some Websites With the Texts

- "America" by Allen Ginsberg: www.writing.upenn.edu/~afilreis/88/america.html
- "Buffalo Soldier" by Bob Marley (Marley & Williams, 1983, side 1 track 2): www.lyricsfreak.com/b/bob+marley/buffalo+soldier_20021701.html
- *Canto General* (*General Song*) by Pablo Neruda (This epic poem fills an entire book, which can be found in most libraries and bookstores. We recommend using sections and especially like those that relate to the history of Chile and other parts of the world [e.g., "Cortes" and "Brother Bartolome de las Casas"].)
- "Do Re Mi" by Woody Guthrie (1940, track 12): www.woodyguthrie.org/Lyrics/Do_Re_Mi.htm
- "Ego Tripping (there may be a reason why)" by Nikki Giovanni: nikki-giovanni.com/page_51.shtml
- "Fear of a Black Planet" by Chuck D (1990, track 12): www.publicenemy.com/index.php?page=page5&item=3&num=75
- "Heart of Hunger" by Martín Espada: www.martinespada.net/heart.htm
- "*Hora 0*" ("Zero Hour") by Ernesto Cardenal: www.poetryfoundation.org/archive/poem.html?id=180094
- "(If You Love Your Uncle Sam) Bring Them Home" by Pete Seeger: www.peteseeger.net/bringthemhome.htm
- "The Lonesome Death of Hattie Carroll" by Bob Dylan (1964, side 2 track 4): www.bobdylan.com/#/songs/lonesome-death-hattie-carroll
- "News Report, September 1991: U.S. Buried Iraqi Soldiers Alive in Gulf War" by Denise Levertov: www.poetryfoundation.org/archive/poem.html?id=180095
- "Problems of Translation: Problems of Language" by June Jordan: www.poetryfoundation.org/archive/poem.html?id=178529
- "Song of Myself" by Walt Whitman: www.princeton.edu/~batke/logr/log_026.html

Ms. Woollven first reads the poem aloud to the class. As she reads, she pauses at certain points to think aloud, highlighting her own reactions to the lines of the poem. For example, she makes note that the repetition of the line, "The other day some one asked me why I write," ties the poem together and pushes it forward. She comments that this poetic device is something she has seen before in other poems, even some the class read earlier in the year. She also stops after the lines, "I write because they made fun of my God / It's not cool to disrespect / so why are you acting like your higher power is the only one that exist / that is nonsense." Here, she discusses the connection she made about turmoil around the world where people of different religions are intolerant of each other. Included in this thought, she reflects on recent post–September 11 examples in the United States in which Muslims have been singled out and harassed simply because they are Muslim.

In her think-aloud, Ms. Woollven highlights the various voices present in the text. She says, "This is interesting, because the poem is written in first person, but there is reference to homeless people, Goth teenagers, people from many religions, gays and lesbians, immigrants in the U.S., and others." She mentions that she felt the poem used many voices to express unity among people and that words can have the power to develop understandings of others. Finally, she comments on the poem's ending by discussing her own feelings of hope and inspiration when reading the closing words, which tie together the multivoiced poem and issue a call for social justice. She explains that the final thought, "I write for purpose / why do you write," seems like a call to readers, challenging them to also pick up a pen and express their thoughts, feelings, and hopes for the world.

After reading the poem to the class, Ms. Woollven instructs students to discuss in small groups various issues brought forth in the text and how such issues relate to their own lives and experiences. Before a whole-class sharing, she invites students to partner talk to encourage them to try out their ideas. She believes that after sharing with one or two others, the students will have the confidence to speak to the larger group. In their small groups, the students discuss their own thoughts about diversity and share opinions about what it was like to be a member of a group often marginalized and excluded from conversations of diversity. In addition to group conversations, the 12th-grade students reflect through journaling and quick-writes, examining social issues in their community and the world that they identify as unjust and in need of attention. In the discussions and journal entries, students bring up numerous issues that are at the forefront of their minds, including gay rights, racism, teen pregnancy, drug abuse, unfair treatment of immigrants, gang violence, gentrification, police brutality, domestic violence, and animal rights. These discussion and writing tasks are a wonderful way to support students' independent thinking.

As students discuss important social issues and reflect on ways to address the associated problems, they continue to examine the poem "Why I Write." They even watch a video of Swain reciting the poem, which can be located on YouTube. Many of the issues presented in the poem overlap with the concerns of the high school students. Ms. Woollven directs the students back to their hard copies of the poem. Next she revisits the lines, thinking aloud as she reads. She starts by saying,

> "The last time I read the poem, we identified repetition as a device used by Tim Swain to move the poem forward. We also talked about the way he incorporated many voices into the text to convey a message of diversity.

Now as I read, let's think about other ways he told a powerful message with word choice and style."

She begins to reread the poem and stops at various places during the reading. After reading the line, "Happy to have this nappy hair that hints what hood I'm from neighbor," she asks the class to comment on what this might mean.

Jasmine states, "He is saying that he is African American."

Ms. Woollven replies, "Hmmm, yes, I think so, too. Okay, but I'm wondering what that means in the context of this sentence? I wonder why it 'hints what hood [he's] from'?"

Anthony replies, "Most neighborhoods are segregated. Just look at Austin. There is a highway, I-35, that divides the city. Mostly all the black and Latino people live on the east side and the white people live on the west. San Antonio is divided up, too."

Ms. Woollven continues with the reading and stops again to ask, "Why do you think he writes, 'excuse me while I steal the sky / I need to wipe my eye with something soft'?"

Again students offer their interpretations. They had done some study of poetry earlier in the year and were familiar with poetic imagery.

Angelo offers this thought, "The voice who is talking just said he lived in a rough neighborhood and it is dangerous and there are thieves. So he is kind of saying life is harsh."

Melissa adds, "Maybe he is wiping his eye, because he shed a tear about the harshness of the place where he lives."

In this way, Ms. Woollven continues through a few more lines, soliciting her students' interpretations as she models questioning the text during a close reading.

Next, she divides the students in groups of four and asks them to continue with a close reading of the rest of the poem to look for ways in which Swain used language to express concern and anger over injustices and present new possibilities for a more just world. Students work in the small groups, keeping a list as they read through the rest of the poem. After they finish, Ms. Woollven gathers the whole class again and the groups share their findings.

They discuss the various stories present in the poem and how each story represents a different voice and social issue. They also note how rhyme was incorporated, although not at the ends of the lines as done in some other poems. They discuss how the writing that Ms. Woollven calls free verse has a certain rhythm and how the rhyming words add to the rhythmic feeling. In addition to rhyme, students note many examples of alliteration. It reminds some students of popular music they listen to, which often tells stories and uses rhyme and alliteration to add to the way the words sound together.

Students also identify examples of allusion when Swain mentions the Easter Bunny, "fat guys from the north pole," Matthew Shepard, and references to football and basketball. Although none of the students remember the term *allusion* from the earlier poetry unit, they are able to discuss how Swain uses cultural and other references to evoke certain meanings, feelings, and images. Ms. Woollven reminds them that this is a poetic device, which scaffolds her students' close reading through her modeling and then through the collaborative groupings in which students are able to put their heads together for the task.

In addition to the study of Swain's poem, the class also embarks on similar close readings of an array of poetry and other text forms, ranging from pieces considered classic, such as Sojourner Truth's 1851 speech "Ain't I a Woman?" and Rodolfo "Corky" Gonzales's poem "I Am Joaquín" (n.d.), to contemporary hip-hop poetry of songwriters such as Lauryn Hill, Tupac Shakur, and Talib Kweli. Each text serves as a mentor text for the students by demonstrating how to express thought and feeling through words. Using ideas adapted from many sources, including the book *Hip-Hop Poetry and the Classics: Connecting Our Classic Curriculum to Hip-Hop Poetry Through Standards-Based, Language Arts Instruction* (Sitomer & Cirelli, 2004), Ms. Woollven leads students through a series of minilessons, examining various forms of poetry and poetic devices, such as alliteration, pattern, imagery, metaphor, hyperbole, personification, symbolism, and imagery.

In one example, she introduces the class to "American Poem," a spoken word poem by Ras Baraka (n.d.). Before giving them the poem, she reminds the students of how Swain used allusion in his poem, again reminding them that this is a common device used in poetry. She tells the class that the next poem they'll be reading also uses allusion. In "American Poem," the poet Baraka creates lists of people and events to symbolize meanings. Ms. Woollven asks the class to consider the title of the poem to predict what imagery they might expect to find in a poem with such a title. The students brainstorm ideas such as apple pie, baseball, democracy, U.S. flags, Christopher Columbus, and the Fourth of July.

Next, she tells the class that this poem also uses a device called irony, which refers to a difference between what is stated and what is actually true. She explains that this poem uses the idea that the U.S. is often depicted in mainstream sources in certain ways that represent the lives and experiences of some segments of society, but other segments are often completely left out. In fact, many events are even left out of traditional history texts that are used in schools. As students connect this idea to the issues brought forth in Swain's poem, they eagerly converse. LaPresha comments that African Americans and Latinos have not traditionally been depicted in a positive light on television and in media, and most of the people who create shows and movies are white. Manuel adds that the story of Columbus is one example that is typically one-sided and that he had seen a show on public television that showed a Native American perspective of the "discovery" of the U.S., and it was very different from what he had learned in school. "Terrific thinking and great connections," says Ms. Woollven, as she acknowledges and encourages the students' ideas by her tone of interaction as well as her words.

Next she explains that in the poem by Baraka, which they were about to read, they would see highlights of a variety of perspectives, people, and events that, like the things they just mentioned, are often overlooked or ignored in mainstream sources. She adds,

> "I believe the sense of irony found in the title also points to the common idea that poems are about 'beautiful' things such as nature and love, but I wonder, *who* has power to determine what is beautiful is often inequitable. Think about this as we share this poem."

Before passing out the text of the poem, Ms. Woollven builds background knowledge by showing a YouTube video clip of the author reciting it on the television show *Russell Simmons Presents Def Poetry*. After watching the video, students discuss the angry tone of the poem. She passes out copies of "American Poem" and asks students to work in pairs to reread it and list all of the events, people, and other images Baraka mentions. She also sets the purpose of the lesson by asking students to think about what symbolism he creates with his lists and why he might have an angry tone. She asks them to jot notes about their thoughts. By sharing multiple texts, she continues to scaffold the students' knowledge.

Students find references to slaves, sharecroppers, ghettos, jazz music, police brutality, "Strange Fruit" (Allan, 1936a), Afro-Cubans, Nuyoricans (Puerto Ricans and those of Puerto Rican descent who live in New York State, particularly the New York City metropolitan area), Joe Hill, Emmett Till, the Ku Klux Klan, and boycotts in Montgomery, Alabama, along with many other references to people of color, diverse cultures, and a history of racism. Students share the lists of images they've compiled from their readings and understand that many of the references relate to people of color who were often excluded from "official" history texts and even mainstream poetry. However, there were many references that the students did not recognize.

Ms. Woollven then has students conduct research on the Internet to get background on the things they were still unsure about. Students discover that "Strange Fruit" (Allan, 1936b, B side) is a song about the lynching of black people in the southern United States, and Joe Hill was a famous union organizer who was put to death for a crime most people believe he did not commit. They also learn that "Dred Scott" refers to the U.S. Supreme Court's 1857 decision in *Dred Scott v. Sandford*, which declared that slaves were not citizens and therefore not protected by the Constitution. Additionally, the students learn that Peekskill, New York, is a city where Paul Robeson sang to crowds of people in support of civil rights. The peaceful concertgoers were attacked by mobs of people who were anti–civil rights, anticommunist members of local organizations, such as the American Legion and Veterans of Foreign Wars, and other local residents, wielding baseball bats and throwing rocks.

Although the tone is angry, and many of the images are of shameful chapters in the nation's history, students also point out that Baraka ends "American Poem" with depictions of "a beautiful black boy" and "a beautiful brown girl," which further add to the idea that representation of people and events has not been equal, and notions of beauty are skewed by those who have the power of authorship. Malik, another student in Ms. Woollven's class, points out that this last point is well illustrated in the final line of the poem, which cries out for a poem of inclusion: "Something that represents me."

The class determines that Swain's poem "Why I Write," Baraka's "American Poem," and the other examples of documentary poems, songs, and speeches they've examined do indeed serve as vehicles for social change. The poems, songs, and speeches not only address important social issues and document injustice, they also serve as educational tools that can inform and inspire others to action. The class acknowledges that they felt moved by many of the examples and even hoped to live life in ways that reflected some of the learning inspired through the documentary-style texts.

Many students comment on the impact they felt after reading the poems. For example, Alexia wrote in her journal,

> I loved the poem Why I Write. In fact, I was so inspired by it that right when I got home, I wrote something on my own. I loved the piece because it reminded me of my own pride and my own dignity.

This reaction was not an isolated one; many students expressed similar reactions in their writing journals. Deshawn wrote, "This makes me want to write poems that intervene into mine and other people's lives and to find what we've all been going through, so I can help others write their own poems." Through content and style, the documentary poems serve as mentor texts; it is as if the poems themselves call out to students and invite them to express their own thoughts about the world around them. This is one of the intended purposes of activist writing and was certainly one of Ms. Woollven's goals when writing the lesson. Further, through purposeful conversational discourse, she is able to understand what the students are learning and thinking, which also authentically supports students' use of academic English.

For the next phase of the lesson, students are challenged to write poetry based on the social justice concerns they identified in their discussions and journaling. Ms. Woollven initiates this with an entry document that she gives to the students, which outlines a scenario that would have them create documentary poetry. The document she created for her students describes the disconnect between young people's knowledge of social, political, and economic issues and their wide-scale apathy and feelings of powerlessness to effect meaningful social change. She challenges the students to voice their concerns about the world in the form of digital poetry with the intention of raising awareness about specific social justice issues. Using the learning from their study of documentary poetry, students are challenged to create their own examples of this poetic form.

Students start with topics from their journaling and model their writing after some of the mentor texts they have studied. In typical writers' workshop fashion, the group of 12th graders brainstorm ideas for prewriting, draft their ideas into poems, share and conference with peers and the teacher, and revise and edit their pieces into finished drafts. Like the mentor texts, students employ an array of poetic devices, such as imagery, metaphors, alliteration, repetition, and rhyming.

Students grapple with social issues and complex problems. They use their knowledge of the world and words to convey authentic feelings about real-world situations. One example by Joey begins, "We'll take a look into the Grand Marquis Police Interceptor edition and from that you tell me where the real criminal is sitting." This student-created poem, a scathing critique of police brutality and abuse of power, focuses on the shooting of Sean Bell in New York by five police officers. Bell and three friends, who were unarmed, were shot a total of 50 times, killing Bell on the morning of what would have been his wedding day. In his poem, Joey captures the tragedy, frustration, and anger over the individual event, and the poem serves as a symbol for the larger issue of police violence. The final lines of the poem captured these feelings while documenting factual information from the case:

> 50 shots fired at a young man with no gun in his waist.
> So the sound of the blue rounds from the officer's gun replaced the
>   wedding bells that were later to come.
> And not one was found responsible...
> I mean guilty.

After writing their pieces, students work to create digital poems. Ms. Woollven shares ideas with students and limits their pieces to two minutes in length to keep the pieces interesting and manageable. First, the class and teacher brainstorm the elements that might be included in a digital poem. Familiar with the form of music videos, students have no problem generating ideas. Their list includes photos, video, scanned art, presentations of the poems via titles or audio recordings, and instrumental music. Next, students use digital poem storyboards (see the Appendix) to plan their poems. The storyboards provide space for students to consider how their visual images will combine with the words of their poem, either in audio voice-overs or text on the screen. Also, instrumental background music can be arranged to provide further emotion to the piece. A digital poem combines modalities to communicate a message. The multimodal format can augment the voice and meaning presented in the piece, but this requires careful planning for intentional effects. The storyboard helps students strategically plan their pieces and sync the various modes of representation. Many books and websites offer in-depth instruction on the technical skills needed to create digital stories and poems using common computer software. Two excellent places to start learning about this writing form are the Llano Grande Center's Captura: Digital Storytelling Toolkit (captura.llanogrande.org) and the Center for Digital Storytelling's Digital Storytelling Cookbook (www.storycenter.org/cookbook.html).

The students create multimodal digital poems using computer software programs such as iMovie and Movie Maker (see Figure 9). A few even explore beyond the technical knowledge of their classroom teacher and use Flash to animate their videos. Regardless of the application used, the students create a layered text that incorporates visual, linguistic, and auditory modes to convey meanings of their poetry. Depending on the topic addressed, students take digital photos, shoot video, or cut and paste images from the Internet to accompany their poems, which were synced to the images using titles or voice-over narrations. Many students also select instrumental tracks to accompany their poems. The digital

Figure 9. Students Working on Documentary Poetry Projects

poems are shared in class as a virtual poetry reading, in which students circulate in groups to view each other's work.

Lesson Example 7: Expository Writing for Advocacy

If classrooms are going to become places for students to practice critical writing and engage transformative intellectuals, as Morrell (2008) suggests, then our writers' workshops must equip young writers with the tools to write in a variety of contexts. Social justice–oriented documentary poetry is one way to tap students' interests in popular culture and remix expository content from social issues with popular forms such as hip-hop and music videos. Another way to channel student interest in social issues and activism is through advocacy writing.

In the book *Reading, Writing, and Rising Up: Teaching About Social Justice and the Power of the Written Word*, Christensen (2000) argues that students must extend their critique of social problems past simply analyzing what is wrong. To stop at analysis would be demoralizing and leave students with a sense of hopelessness and doom. Critical writing in the classroom is intended to help students develop agency as participants of democracy and therefore feel the power to act on issues they identify as problematic. Expository writing for advocacy is simply a way for students to focus energy on disseminating information with the intentions of education and activism.

Expository Writing for Advocacy Overview

Students in Ms. Woollven's language arts class learn about this style of nonfiction writing during their unit focusing on poetry and social justice. Spinning off the topics of their poems, students work in groups to narrow their topics and conduct research on related issues. Their writing project extends from a traditional research summary to a media report designed to educate others about their chosen social justice topic. The following steps provide a brief overview to a lesson that guides students in advocacy writing:

1. Group students based on similarities of interests as deemed by their documentary poetry topics. Together the group members narrow their topic to one focus issue. (collaborative teamwork)

2. The students in each group work together to conduct research on their chosen topic. They write a group research summary including references. (collaborative learning)

3. Each group creates media to raise public awareness about their topics. (independence)

4. The groups take turns presenting the media to the class. (collaborative learning)

Expository Writing for Advocacy in Action

The focus on documentary poetry helps generate interest among students about a broad spectrum of social concerns. While creating and then sharing their digital poems with the class, students see that there are many parallel interests and concerns among their peers. Ms. Woollven recognizes the importance of tapping the students' interests and social awareness and guides them to seek ways to act as change agents through their writing. She, like many other critical writing teachers, believes in the importance of writing curriculum that not only identifies social problems but also teaches young writers about democratic civic engagement.

Using a gradual release model of instruction with the goal of student independence, Ms. Woollven designed a lesson for groups of students to conduct further research on a selected social issue and then create media to raise public awareness. She begins by grouping students with similar interests based on their documentary poetry topics chosen earlier, including environmental issues, teen suicide, drug and alcohol abuse, neglect of children, and various humanitarian issues around the world. She then provides the groups with the following instructions:

> Based on the ideas and concerns reflected in your digital poems, the Social Action Collective's political arm, SAC PAC, has assigned you to an action committee responsible for raising public awareness regarding a social justice issue and proposing an action plan for effecting change. Your media presentations may include documentaries, television or radio commercials, or television news programs. Presentations must be accompanied by reference summaries and a works cited page listing those references. Action committees must present the issue with honesty and integrity—it is the job of the committee to ensure that the public has a full understanding of the issue, current government policy, the causes of the issue, and the plan for action being proposed by the committee. Action committees must consider societal attitudes toward the issue, expert opinions, and current or needed government policies regarding the issue.

Each group is responsible for discussing their ideas for focal topics and narrowing the ideas to one social issue for their media presentation project. Together the teams conduct background research using Internet and library sources.

Because Ms. Woollven recognizes the need for students to gain skills in traditional print literacies as well as the new literacies, she includes a research paper as part of the assignment leading up to the media report. Students are guided to write summaries of their research findings that relate to their topics based on a framework provided by the teacher. Ms. Woollven earlier prepared a research paper outline template to scaffold the students' organization of ideas (see the Appendix). Each report should be divided into six sections: an introduction, an overview of the issue, different perspectives on the issue, related laws and regulations, recommendations for change, and a conclusion. The template guides students through each of the sections by providing guidance about the number of paragraphs required and suggestions for the type of information that would be relevant.

One group focuses on the issue of the "invisible children" of Uganda, who are young people kidnapped and forced to become soldiers in the country's civil war that has been going on for over 20 years. The group describes the problem and identifies a number of organizations dedicated to assisting the victims of this horrible situation. One of the organizations includes a local branch of the Invisible Children awareness campaign run by students in this high school. The Invisible Children campaign began when some students at the University of San Diego made a documentary about the war in Uganda, highlighting the great human suffering that the war has inflicted, especially among children who are often forced to become soldiers. In response to the movie, many people have donated money and time to help provide needed resources to the children of central Africa. Students in high schools and universities across the United States have become involved in this campaign, which began with the short documentary. This group in Ms. Woollven's class sold bracelets and informational DVDs to other students and members of the school community, donating all proceeds for the education of Ugandan children. They conclude their paper with a call to action:

> There are many creative ways to help. Possibly the easiest is to raise awareness on the issue of invisible children and making people realize the horrors and abominations that are taking place in northern Uganda. Another thing you can do to help is to make a donation by buying a bracelet or the DVD or a t-shirt. Or you yourself can come up with creative ways to help, maybe starting a fundraiser in school, church, or work, gathering clothing, food, toys, blankets, pillows, bedding. Anything can help in Northern Uganda.

Through their research efforts, Ms. Woollven's students gain important information on their topics. They gather data from multiple sources and synthesize the information in their research summaries. In addition, these research reports help the students articulate ideas for civic engagement to enact positive social change on local and global levels. These ideas for action are at the heart of critical literacy curriculum. Having students research social problems cannot stop at analysis of the problem or we run the risk of demoralizing students and generating classrooms of cynicism. When students engage in problem solving, they learn about agency and collaboration in the name of social justice.

Springboarding off their own research papers, the groups embark on efforts to create media to raise public awareness around their focal issues. Groups are given the open-ended task of creating media for advocacy. They are offered choices in the modes and mediums for their presentations. Ms. Woollven suggests that students select between mock television or radio commercials, documentaries, or the creation of websites. Students have access to classroom tools, including computers and digital cameras.

Students work together to plan and produce their media projects. Figure 10 shows a group of students editing a documentary about the environment. One group of students use Movie Maker and other video editing software to communicate their message about respect for the environment. They include still photographs that they took, images found on the Internet, and video clips they shot at school. The visual images are accompanied by an audio track that includes voice-over narration, providing facts and figures learned during the group research as well as suggestions for ways viewers can act to make a difference in their communities (see Figure 11).

Although the examples of media advocacy created by Ms. Woollven's students are never aired on real television or radio outlets, the student-created media are presented to the class. In this way, students' advocacy efforts reach a broader audience and initiate further discussion in class and around the school. Through the experience of creating the expository media texts, students learn important lessons about making their voices heard in a democratic society. This is a first step toward expanding their participation as critically literate citizens.

Figure 10. Students Working on Media for Advocacy Writing

Figure 11. Images From a Student Group's Advocacy Documentary on the Environment

Using Remix to Engage Students' Writing in the Classroom

The students in Ms. Woollven's 12th-grade language arts class learn about writing for authentic purposes to inform, express positions, and call others to action. In other words, the students who engage in the lessons depicted in this chapter learn to view writing as *the* tool for social change (Morrell, 2008). By analyzing mentor texts, continuing to the creation of their own multimodal writing projects documenting social injustices, and then taking advocacy stances, students practice critical writing as a form of civic participation.

Although there are many new ways for people to express meaning, the need to teach students to write using traditional, print-based literacy in standard language continues to be of utmost importance in our schools. Therefore, so-called "old literacies" of grammar, punctuation, and standard language practices are necessary in our classrooms, and the activities shared in the chapter show how Ms. Woollven incorporates traditional print literacies into the writing workshop.

However, the need for continued emphasis on traditional, print-based literacy need not come at the expense of incorporation of new literacies. In fact, we believe that the two are complementary and necessary companions in today's classrooms. Students in Ms. Woollven's language arts classroom fluidly move from traditional-style research papers to digital projects to print-based poetry to more digital projects. Not only are both styles of writing valid and extremely useful for 21st-century citizens but also more options provide increased means and mediums for expression of more complex thoughts. For these reasons, the remix of old and new forms of writing is essential for language arts classrooms today.

Reproducibles

Storyboard for a Montage Sequence

Name: _____

Images

Narration, Titles, and Audio

Notes on How Images Collide

Literacy Remix: Bridging Adolescents' In and Out of School Literacies by Jesse Gainer and Diane Lapp. © 2010 by the International Reading Association.

Storyboard for Digital Poems

Title of Poem: _____

Visual Images				
Text and Titles				
Voice-Over Narration				
Instrumental Music and Other Audio				

Research Paper Outline Template

Group Members: _____

_____

Social Justice Issue: _____

I. Introduction (This is usually one paragraph.)

    A. Thesis Statement (This is usually included in the introductory paragraph, but does not have to be its first sentence.): _____

_____

    B. Essay Map (This is a summary of the major points that you will make in your essay, so you should write a brief summary of sections II, III, IV, and V here.)

        1. _____

        2. _____

        3. _____

        4. _____

II. Description of Issue (This will probably be two or three paragraphs.)

    A. Issue:_____

        1. _____

        2. _____

        3. _____

    B. Causes

        1. _____

        2. _____

        3. _____

    C. Effects

        1. _____

        2. _____

        3. _____

III. Public Opinion and Various Perspectives on Issue (This will probably be two or three paragraphs.)

    A. Perspective/Side 1: _____

        1. _____

        2. _____

    B. Perspective/Side 2: _____

        1. _____

        2. _____

(continued)

Literacy Remix: Bridging Adolescents' In and Out of School Literacies by Jesse Gainer and Diane Lapp.
© 2010 by the International Reading Association.

Research Paper Outline Template (*continued*)

C. Public Awareness (This could include professional or student-generated polls and surveys.)

    1. _____

    2. _____

IV. Government Policies, Regulations, and/or Laws (This will probably be two or three paragraphs.)

  A. _____

    1. _____

    2. _____

  B. _____

    1. _____

    2. _____

  C. _____

    1. _____

    2. _____

V. Recommendations for Change (This will probably be one or two paragraphs and will drive your group's media presentation. You may want to include how to raise awareness, how people's attitudes and beliefs need to change, and finally, specific action to be taken by individuals, groups, or governments to make change happen. How can your group influence individuals, groups, or governments?)

  A. _____

    1. _____

    2. _____

  B. _____

    1. _____

    2. _____

  C. _____

    1. _____

    2. _____

VI. Conclusion (This should be one paragraph that restates your thesis and summarizes how you have proven it with the evidence in your paper.)

  A. _____

  B. _____

  C. _____

  D. _____

Literacy Remix: Bridging Adolescents' In and Out of School Literacies by Jesse Gainer and Diane Lapp. © 2010 by the International Reading Association.

REFERENCES

Afflerbach, P., Pearson, P.D., & Paris, S.G. (2008). Clarifying differences between reading skills and reading strategies. *The Reading Teacher, 61*(5), 364–373. doi:10.1598/RT.61.5.1

Alvermann, D.E., & Heron, A.H. (2001). Literacy identity work: Playing to learn with popular media. *Journal of Adolescent & Adult Literacy, 45*(2), 118–122.

Alvermann, D.E., Moon, J.S., & Hagood, M.C. (1999). *Popular culture in the classroom: Teaching and researching critical media literacy.* Newark, DE: International Reading Association; Chicago: National Reading Conference.

Anderson, R.C., & Pearson, P.D. (1984). A schema-theoretic view of basic processes in reading comprehension. In P.D. Pearson, R. Barr, M.L. Kamil, & P. Mosenthal (Eds.), *Handbook of reading research* (pp. 255–291). White Plains, NY: Longman.

Bailey, A.L., & Heritage, M. (2008). *Formative assessment for literacy, grades K–6: Building reading and academic language skills across the curriculum.* Thousand Oaks, CA: Corwin.

Ball, A.F., & Farr, M. (2003). Language varieties, culture and teaching the English language arts. In J. Flood, D. Lapp, J.R. Squire, & J.M. Jensen (Eds.), *Handbook of research on teaching the English language arts* (2nd ed., pp. 435–445). Mahwah, NJ: Erlbaum.

Bean, T.W. (2000). Reading in the content areas: Social constructivist dimensions. In M.L. Kamil, P.B. Mosenthal, P.D. Pearson, & R. Barr (Eds.), *Handbook of reading research* (Vol. 3, pp. 629–644). Mahwah, NJ: Erlbaum.

Beck, I., McKeown, M., & Kucan, L. (2002). *Bringing words to life: Robust vocabulary instruction.* New York: Guilford.

Biancarosa, G., & Snow, C.E. (2004). *Reading next—A vision for action and research in middle and high school literacy: A report to Carnegie Corporation of New York.* Washington, DC: Alliance for Excellent Education.

Black, R.W. (2005). *Online fanfiction: What technology and popular culture can teach us about writing and literacy instruction.* New Horizons for Learning. Retrieved September 26, 2009, from www.newhorizons.org/strategies/literacy/black.htm

Brock, C., Lapp, D., Salas, R., & Townsend, D. (Eds.). (2009). *Learning to converse, conversing to learn: Instruction that helps English language learners develop academic language proficiency.* New York: Teachers College Press.

Brookfield, S.D. (1995). *Becoming a critically reflective teacher.* San Francisco: Jossey-Bass.

Brown, A.L., & Campione, J.C. (1981). Inducing flexible thinking: A problem of access. In M.P. Friedman, J.P. Das, & N. O'Connor (Eds.), *Intelligence and learning* (pp. 515–529). New York: Plenum.

Chamot, A.U., & O'Malley, J.M. (1989). The cognitive academic language learning approach. In P. Rigg & V.G. Allen (Eds.), *When they don't all speak English: Integrating the ESL student into the regular classroom* (pp. 108–125). Urbana, IL: National Council of Teachers of English.

Christensen, L. (2000). *Reading, writing, and rising up: Teaching about social justice and the power of the written word.* Milwaukee, WI: Rethinking Schools.

Coiro, J. (2003). Rethinking comprehension strategies to better prepare students for critically evaluating content on the Internet. *The New England Reading Association Journal, 39*(2), 29–34.

Coiro, J., Knobel, M., Lankshear, C., & Leu, D.J. (2008). *Handbook of research on new literacies.* New York: Routledge.

Comber, B., & Nixon, H. (2005). Children reread and rewrite their local neighborhoods: Critical literacies and identity work. In J. Evans (Ed.), *Literacy moves on: Popular culture, new technologies, and critical literacy in the elementary classroom* (pp. 127–148). Portsmouth, NH: Heinemann.

Davis, F.B. (1944). Fundamental factors of comprehension in reading. *Psychometrika, 9*(3), 185–197. doi:10.1007/BF02288722

Delpit, L. (1988). The silenced dialogue: Power and pedagogy in educating other people's children. *Harvard Educational Review, 58*(3), 280–298.

Delpit, L. (1995). *Other people's children: Cultural conflict in the classroom.* New York: New Press.

Delpit, L., & Dowdy, J.K. (Eds.). (2002). *The skin that we speak: Thoughts on language and culture in the classroom.* New York: New Press.

Deschenes, S., Cuban, L., & Tyack, D. (2001). Mismatch: Historical perspectives on schools and students who don't fit them. *Teachers College Record, 103*(4), 525–547. doi: 10.1111/0161-4681.00126

Deschler, D.D., Palincsar, A.S., Biancarosa, G., & Nair, M. (2007). *Informed choices for struggling adolescent readers: A research-based guide to instructional programs and practices.* Newark, DE: International Reading Association.

Dowdall, C. (2006). Dissonance between the digitally created words of school and home. *Literacy, 40*(3), 153–163.

Duke, N.K., & Pearson, P.D. (2002). Effective practices for developing reading comprehension. In A.E. Farstrup & S.J. Samuels (Eds.), *What research has to say about reading instruction* (3rd ed., pp. 205–242). Newark, DE: International Reading Association.

Eagleton, M.B., & Dobler, E. (2007). *Reading the Web: Strategies for Internet inquiry.* New York: Guilford.

Edwards, P.A. (2007, November). *The education of African American students: Voicing the debates, controversies, and solutions.* Presidential address presented at the National Reading Conference, Austin, TX.

Engeström, Y. (2008). *From teams to knots: Active-theoretical studies of collaboration and learning at work.* New York: Cambridge University Press.

Fisher, D., & Frey, N. (2003). Writing instruction for struggling adolescent readers: A gradual release model. *Journal of Adolescent & Adult Literacy, 46*(5), 396–405.

Fisher, D., & Frey, N. (2008). *Better learning through structured teaching: A framework for the gradual release of responsibility.* Alexandria, VA: Association for Supervision and Curriculum Development.

Fisher, D., Frey, N., & Lapp, D. (2009). *In a reading state of mind: Brain research, teacher modeling, and comprehension instruction.* Newark, DE: International Reading Association.

Fisher, D., & Ivey, G. (2007). Farewell to *A Farewell to Arms*: Deemphasizing the whole-class novel. *Phi Delta Kappan, 88*(7), 494–497.

Franzak, J.K. (2006). Zoom: A review of the literature on marginalized adolescent readers, literacy theory, and policy implications. *Review of Educational Research, 76*(2), 209–248. doi:10.3102/00346543076002209

Freire, P. (1970). *Pedagogy of the oppressed.* New York: Continuum.

Freire, P., & Macedo, D. (1987). *Literacy: Reading the word and the world.* South Hadley, MA: Bergin & Garvey.

Gay, G. (2002). Preparing for culturally responsive teaching. *Journal of Teacher Education, 53*(2), 106–116. doi:10.1177/0022487102053002003

Gee, J. (1996). *Social linguistics and literacies: Ideology in discourses.* New York: RoutledgeFalmer.

Goleman, D. (2009). *Ecological intelligence: How knowing the hidden impacts of what we buy can change everything.* New York: Broadway Books.

González, N., Moll, L.C., & Amanti, C. (Eds.). (2004). *Funds of knowledge: Theorizing practices in households, communities, and classrooms.* Mahwah, NJ: Erlbaum.

Guthrie, J.T., & Humenick, N.M. (2004). Motivating students to read: Evidence for classroom practices that increase reading motivation and achievement. In P. McCardle & V. Chhabra (Eds.), *The voice of evidence in reading research* (pp. 329–354). Baltimore: Paul H. Brookes.

Guthrie, J.T., & Wigfield, A. (2000). Engagement and motivation in reading. In M.L. Kamil, P.B. Mosenthal, P.D. Pearson, & R. Barr (Eds.), *Handbook of reading research* (Vol. 3, pp. 403–422). Mahwah, NJ: Erlbaum.

Gutiérrez, K., & Lee, C.D (2009). Robust informal learning environments for youth from nondominant groups: Implications for literacy learning in formal schooling. In L.M. Morrow, R. Rueda, & D. Lapp (Eds.), *Handbook of research on literacy and diversity* (pp. 216–232). New York: Guilford.

Gutiérrez, K.D., Baquedano-Lopez, P., & Turner, M.G. (1997). Putting language back into language arts: When the radical middle meets the third space. *Language Arts, 74*(5), 368–378.

Halliday, M.A.K. (1994). *An introduction to functional grammar* (2nd ed.). London: Hodder Arnold.

Hart, B., & Risley, T.R. (1995). *Meaningful differences in the everyday experience of young American children.* Baltimore: Paul H. Brookes.

Heath, S.B. (1983). *Ways with words: Language, life, and work in communities and classrooms.* Cambridge, England: Cambridge University Press.

Heath, S.B. (1991). The sense of being literate: Historical and cross-cultural features. In R. Barr, M.L. Kamil, P.B. Mosenthal, & P.D. Pearson (Eds.), *Handbook of reading research* (Vol. 2, pp. 3–25). White Plains, NY: Longman.

Hirsch, E.D., Jr. (1987). *Cultural literacy: What every American needs to know.* Boston: Houghton Mifflin.

Hymes, D. (1972). Models of the interaction of language and social life. In J.J. Gumperz & D. Hymes (Eds.), *Directions in sociolinguistics: The ethnography of communication* (pp. 35–71). New York: Holt, Rinehart & Winston.

International Reading Association & National Council of Teachers of English. (1996). *Standards for the English language arts.* Newark, DE; Urbana, IL: Authors.

Israel, S.E., & Duffy, G.G. (Eds.). (2008). *Handbook of research on reading comprehension.* New York: Routledge.

Ivey, G. (2008, October). *Making up for lost time: Connecting inexperienced teenage readers with books.* Paper presented at the Ball Foundation Family Literacy Symposium, Chicago.

Ivey, G., & Broaddus, K. (2001). "Just plain reading": A survey of what makes students want to read in middle school classrooms. *Reading Research Quarterly, 36*(4), 350–377. doi:10.1598/RRQ.36.4.2

Ivey, G., & Broaddus, K. (2007). A formative experiment investigating literacy engagement among adolescent Latina/o students just beginning to read, write, and speak English. *Reading Research Quarterly, 42*(4), 512–545. doi: 10.1598/RRQ.42.4.4

Johnston, P.H. (2004). *Choice words: How our language affects children's learning.* Portland, ME: Stenhouse.

Keller, D. (2008). The musician as thief: Digital culture and copyright law. In P.D. Miller (Ed.), *Sound unbound: Sampling digital music and culture* (pp. 135–150). Cambridge, MA: MIT Press.

Kesten, C. (1987). *Independent learning: A common essential learning.* Regina, Canada: Saskatchewan Education.

Kist, W. (2005). *New literacies in action: Teaching and learning in multiple media.* New York: Teachers College Press.

Klein, N. (2002). *No logo: No space, no choice, no jobs* (2nd ed.). New York: Picador.

Knobel, M., & Lankshear, C. (2008). Remix: The art and craft of endless hybridization. *Journal of Adolescent & Adult Literacy, 52*(1), 22–33. doi: 10.1598/ JAAL.52.1.3

Kucan, L., & Beck, I.L. (1997). Thinking aloud and reading comprehension research: Inquiry, instruction, and social interaction. *Review of Educational Research, 67*(3), 271–299.

Labbo, L.D. (2006). Literacy pedagogy and computer technologies: Toward solving the puzzle of current and future classroom practices. *Australian Journal of Language and Literacy, 29*(3), 199–209.

Labov, W. (1972). *Language in the inner city: Studies in the black English vernacular.* Philadelphia: University of Pennsylvania Press.

Lankshear, C., & Knobel, M. (2002). Do we have your attention? New literacies, digital technologies, and the education of adolescents. In D.E. Alvermann (Ed.), *Adolescents and literacies in a digital world* (pp. 19–39). New York: Peter Lang.

Lankshear, C., & Knobel, M. (2006). *New literacies: Everyday practices and classroom learning* (2nd ed.). Maidenhead, Berkshire, England: Open University Press.

Lapp, D., & Fisher, D. (2009). It's all about the book: Motivating teens to read. *Journal of Adolescent & Adult Literacy, 52*(7), 556–561. doi: 10.1598/JAAL.52.7.1

Lee, C.D. (2006). "Every good-bye ain't gone": Analyzing the cultural underpinnings of classroom talk. *International Journal of Qualitative Studies in Education, 19*(3), 305–327.

Lee, J., Grigg, W.S., & Donahue, P.L. (2007). *The nation's report card: Reading 2007: National assessment of educational progress at grades 4 and 8* (NCES No. 2007–496). Washington, DC: National Center for Education Statistics, Institute of Education Sciences, U.S. Department of Education.

Leu, D.J., Jr., Kinzer, C.K., Coiro, J., & Cammack, D.W. (2004). Toward a theory of new literacies emerging from the Internet and other information and communication technologies. In R.B. Ruddell & N.J. Unrau (Eds.), *Theoretical models and processes of reading* (5th ed., pp. 1570–1613). Newark, DE: International Reading Association.

Mahiri, J. (Ed.). (2004). *What they don't learn in school: Literacy in the lives of urban youth.* New York: Peter Lang.

Marzano, R.J. (2004). *Building background knowledge for academic achievement: Research on what works in schools.* Alexandria, VA: Association for Supervision and Curriculum Development.

Merchant, G. (2001). Teenagers in cyberspace: An investigation of language use and language change in Internet chatrooms. *Journal of Research in Reading, 24*(3), 293–306.

Metres, P. (2009). *From Reznikoff to Public Enemy: The poet as journalist, historian, agitator.* Retrieved June 18, 2009, from www.poetryfoundation.org/journal/article.html?id=180213

Moore, D.W., Bean, T.W., Birdyshaw, D., & Rycik, J.A. (1999). *Adolescent literacy: A position statement for the Commission on Adolescent Literacy of the International Reading Association.* Newark, DE: International Reading Association.

Moran, J., Ferdig, R.E., Pearson, P.D., Wardrop, J., & Blomeyer, R.L., Jr. (2008). Technology and reading performance in the middle-school grades: A meta-analysis with recommendations for policy and practice. *Journal of Literacy Research, 40*(1), 6–58.

Morrell, E. (2008). *Critical literacy and urban youth: Pedagogics of access, dissent, and liberation.* New York: Routledge.

Morrell, E., & Duncan-Andrade, J. (2002). Toward a critical classroom discourse: Promoting academic literacy through engaging hip-hop culture with urban youth. *English Journal, 91*(6), 88–94.

National Council of Teachers of English. (2008). *Code of best practices in fair use for media literacy education.* Retrieved April 21, 2009, from www.ncte.org/positions/statements/fairusemedialiteracy

New London Group, The. (1996). A pedagogy of multiliteracies: Designing social futures. *Harvard Educational Review, 66*(1), 60–92.

Ostenson, J. (2009). Skeptics on the Internet: Teaching students to read critically. *English Journal, 98*(5), 54–59.

Paris, S.G., Lipson, M.Y., & Wixson, K.K. (1983). Becoming a strategic reader. *Contemporary Educational Psychology, 8*(3), 293–316. doi:10.1016/0361-476X(83)90018-8

Pearson, P.D., & Gallagher, M.C. (1983). The instruction of reading comprehension. *Contemporary Educational Psychology, 8*(3), 317–344. doi:10.1016/0361-476X(83)90019-X

Pincus, E., & Ascher, S. (1984). *The filmmaker's handbook*. New York: Penguin.

Prensky, M. (2001). Digital natives, digital immigrants [Electronic version]. *On the Horizon, 9*(5), 1–6.

Prensky, M. (2005). Listen to the natives. *Educational Leadership, 63*(4), 8–13.

Pressley, M. (2000). What should comprehension instruction be the instruction of? In M.L. Kamil, P.B. Mosenthal, P.D. Pearson, & R. Barr (Eds.), *Handbook of reading research* (Vol. 3, pp. 545–561). Mahwah, NJ: Erlbaum.

Pressley, M., Johnson, C.J., Symons, S., McGoldrick, J.A., & Kurita, J.A. (1989). Strategies that improve children's memory and comprehension of text. *The Elementary School Journal, 90*(1), 3–32. doi:10.1086/461599

Pring-Mill, R. (1980). The redemption of reality through documentary poetry [Introductory essay]. In E. Cardenal, *Zero hour and other documentary poems* (pp. ix–xxi). New York: New Directions.

Ravitch, D. (2003). *The language police: How pressure groups restrict what students learn*. New York: Knopf.

Rose, T. (1994). *Black noise: Rap music and black culture in contemporary America*. Middletown, CT: Wesleyan University Press.

Schallert, D.L., & Reed, J.H. (1997). The pull of the text and the process of involvement in reading. In J.T. Guthrie & A. Wigfield (Eds.), *Reading engagement: Motivating readers through integrated instruction* (pp. 68–85). Newark, DE: International Reading Association.

Scherff, L., & Piazza, C. (2005). The more things change, the more they stay the same: A survey of high school students' writing experiences. *Research in the Teaching of English, 39*(3), 271–304.

Selfe, C.L., & Hawisher, G.E. (2004). *Literate lives in the Information Age: Narratives of literacy from the United States* (p. 233). Mahwah, NJ: Erlbaum.

Shamburg, C. (2008). *English language arts units for grades 9–12*. Eugene, OR: International Society for Technology in Education.

Sitomer, A., & Cirelli, M. (2004). *Hip-hop poetry and the classics: Connecting our classic curriculum to hip-hop poetry through standards-based, language arts instruction*. Beverly Hills, CA: Milk Mug.

Smitherman, G. (1977). *Talkin and testifyin: The language of black America*. Boston: Houghton Mifflin.

Smitherman, G. (2000). *Talking that talk: Language, culture, and education in African America*. New York: Routledge.

Stahl, S.A. (2005). Four problems with teaching word meanings (and what to do to make vocabulary an integral part of instruction). In E.H. Hiebert & M.L. Kamil (Eds.), *Teaching and learning vocabulary: Bringing research to practice* (pp. 95–114). Mahwah, NJ: Erlbaum.

Sutherland, L.M., Botzakis, S., Moje, E.B., & Alvermann, D.E. (2008). Drawing on youth cultures in content learning and literacy. In D. Lapp, J. Flood, & N. Farnan (Eds.), *Content area reading and learning: Instructional strategies* (3rd ed., pp. 133–156). Mahwah, NJ: Erlbaum.

Swadener, B.B. (1995). Children and families "at promise": Deconstructing the discourse of risk. In B.B. Swadener & S. Lubeck (Eds.), *Children and families* "at promise": Deconstructing the discourse of risk (pp. 17–49). Albany: State University of New York Press.

Torgesen, J.K., Houston, D.D., Rissman, L.M., Decker, S.M., Roberts, G., Vaughn, S., et al. (2007). *Academic literacy instruction for adolescents: A guidance document from the Center on Instruction.* Portsmouth, NH: RMC Research Corporation, Center on Instruction.

Turner, K.H. (2009). Flipping the switch: Code switching from text speak to Standard English. *English Journal, 98*(5), 60–65.

Vasquez, V.M. (2004). *Negotiating critical literacies with young children.* Mahwah, NJ: Erlbaum.

Vygotsky, L.S. (1962). *Thought and language* (E. Hanfmann & G. Vakar, Eds. & Trans.). Cambridge, MA: MIT Press.

Vygotsky, L.S. (1978). *Mind in society: The development of higher psychological processes* (M. Cole, V. John-Steiner, S. Scribner, & E. Souberman, Eds. & Trans.). Cambridge, MA: Harvard University Press.

Wikipedia. (n.d.). Remix. Retrieved July 2009 from en.wikipedia.org/wiki/Remix

Wolfram, W., Adger, C.T., & Christian, D. (1999). *Dialects in schools and communities.* Mahwah, NJ: Erlbaum.

Yagelski, R.P. (2005). Stasis and change: English education and the crisis of sustainability. *English Education, 37*(4), 262–271.

Zhang, P. (2009, May). Theorizing the relationship between affect and aesthetics in the ICT design and use context. *Proceedings of the International Conference on Information Resource Management, Dubai, United Arab Emirates.* Retrieved April 9, 2009, from melody.syr.edu/pzhang/publications/CIRM_09_Zhang_Affect_Aesthetics.pdf

Aleksandrov, G. (Director), & Eisenstein, S. (Director). (1928). *October: Ten days that shook the world* [Motion picture]. Soviet Union: Sovkino.

Allan, L. [Abel Meeropol]. (1936a). Strange fruit [Poem]. *New York Teacher.*

Allan, L. [Abel Meeropol]. (1936b). Strange fruit [Recorded by Billie Holiday as a single]. United States: Commodore. (Recorded 1939)

Baraka, R. (n.d.). *American poem* [Spoken word poem]. Retrieved November 23, 2009, from www.youtube.com/watch?v=-m7M8LeEpFc

Beatles, The. (1968). *The Beatles* [Record]. London, England: EMI.

Berlanga, G., & Canut, I. (2002). ¿A quién le importa? [Recorded by Thalía]. On *Thalía* [CD]. Miami, FL: EMI Latin.

Brumley, A.E. (1929). I'll fly away [Melody sampled by Puff Daddy & Faith Evans in I'll be missing you]. On *No way out* [CD]. New York: Bad Boy Records.

Carter, S., & West, K. (2003). Encore [Recorded by Jay-Z]. On *The black album* [CD]. New York: Roc-A-Fella & Def Jam Records.

Chartoff, R. (Producer), Winkler, I. (Producer), & Avildsen, J. (Director). (1976). *Rocky* [Motion picture]. United States: United Artists.

Chicago Blues All Stars. (1970). Introduction. On *American Folk Blues Festival '70* [Record]. Germany: L+R Records. Retrieved October 30, 2009, from mp3.rhapsody.com/album/american-folk-blues-festival-70--1989?artistId= art.41918

D, C. (1990). Fear of a black planet [Recorded by Public Enemy]. On *Fear of a black planet* [CD]. United States: Def Jam & Columbia Records. (Recorded 1989)

Danger Mouse. (2004). *The grey album* [Record]. United States: record label unknown.

Danger Mouse (Producer). (n.d.). *The grey video* [Video]. Retrieved October 26, 2009, from www.youtube.com/watch?v=3zJqihkLcGc

Dylan, B. (1964). The Lonesome Death of Hattie Carroll. On *The times they are a-changin'* [Record]. United States: Columbia Records. (Recorded 1964)

Gonzales, R.C. (n.d.). *I am Joaquín* [Poem]. Retrieved November 19, 2009, from www.latinamericanstudies.org/latinos/joaquin.htm

Guthrie, W. (1940). Do re mi. On *Dust bowl ballads* [Record]. United States: RCA Victor.

Hahn, D. (Producer), Allers, R. (Director), & Minkoff, R. (Director). (1994). *The lion king* [Motion picture]. United States: Walt Disney Pictures.

Hansberry, L. (1959/2004). *A raisin in the sun.* New York: Vintage.

Hughes, J. (Producer/Director), & Tanen, N. (Producer). (1985). *The breakfast club* [Motion picture]. United States: Universal Studios.

Hughes, J.L. (1951). Harlem [Poem]. In *Montage of a dream deferred.* New York: Holt. Retrieved November 9, 2009, from www.cswnet.com/~menamc/langston.htm

Hughes, J.L. (1998). I, too, sing America [Poem written 1925]. In C. Clinton & S. Alcorn (Eds.), *I, too, sing America: Three centuries of African American poetry* (p. 9). New York: Houghton Mifflin.

Hughes, J.L., & Hurston, Z.N. (1930/1991). *Mule bone: A comedy of Negro life.* New York: HarperCollins.

Hurston, Z.N. (1937). *Their eyes were watching God.* Philadelphia: Lippincott.

Hurston, Z.N. (2000). How it feels to be colored me [Poem written 1928]. In J.C. Oates (Ed.), *The best American essays of the century* (pp. 114–117). Boston: Houghton Mifflin.

Jay-Z. (2003). *The black album* [CD]. New York: Roc-A-Fella & Def Jam Records.

King, E., Rock, K., Rossington, G., Kracker, U., Van Zant, R., Watchel, R., et al. (2007). All summer long [Recorded by Kid Rock]. On *Rock n roll Jesus* [CD]. Nashville, TN: Atlantic.

King, E., Rossington, G., & Van Zant, R. (1974). Sweet home Alabama [Recorded by Lynyrd Skynyrd]. On *Second helping* [Record]. Doraville, GA: MCA. (Recorded 1973)

King, M.L., Jr. (1963, August 28). *I have a dream: Address at March on Washington* [Speech]. Retrieved November 16, 2009, from www.mlkonline .net/dream.html

Leonard, A. (n.d.). *The story of stuff with Annie Leonard* [Website]. Retrieved May 10, 2009, from www.storyofstuff.com

Marinell, L., Wachtel, R., & Zevon, W. (1978). Werewolves of London [Recorded by Warren Zevon]. On *Excitable boy* [Record]. Los Angeles: Asylum Records. (Recorded 1977)

Marley, B., & Tosh, P. (1990). Get up, stand up [Recorded by Bob Marley and the Wailers]. On *Legend: The Best of Bob Marley and the Wailers* [CD]. New York: Tuff Gong Records. (Recorded 1973)

Marley, B., & Williams, N.G. (1983). Buffalo soldier [Recorded by Bob Marley and the Wailers]. On *Confrontation* [Record]. New York: Tuff Gong & Island Records.

Negativland (Producer). (2007). *Our favorite things* [DVD]. United States: Seeland.

Shenson, W. (Producer), & Lester, R. (Director). (1964). *A hard day's night* [Motion picture]. United Kingdom: United Artists.

Sting. (1983). Every breath you take [Recorded by The Police]. On *Synchronicity* [CD]. Santa Monica, CA: A&M Records. (Recorded 1982)

Sting, Gaither, T., & Evans, F. (1997). I'll be missing you [Recorded by Puff Daddy & Faith Evans]. On *No way out* [CD]. New York: Bad Boy Records.

Swain, T. (n.d.). *Why I write* [Spoken word poem]. Retrieved November 23, 2009, from www.dailymotion.com/video/x330nt_why-i-write-final-01windows-media-v_politics

Truth, S. (1851). *Ain't I a woman?* [Speech delivered at the Women's Convention in Akron, OH]. Retrieved November 19, 2009, from www.feminist.com/ resources/artspeech/genwom/sojour.htm

Welles, O. (Producer/Director). (1941). *Citizen Kane* [Motion picture]. United States: RKO Pictures.

will.i.am (Producer), Jurkovac, M. (Producer), & Dylan, J. (Director). (2008). *Yes we can* [Video]. Retrieved October 26, 2009, from www.youtube.com/ watch?v=SsV2O4fCgjk

Wise, R. (Producer/Director). (1965). *The sound of music* [Motion picture]. United States: 20th Century Fox.

INDEX

Note. Page numbers followed by *f* and *t* indicate figures and tables, respectively.

9744

storyboard: for digital poems, 103; for montage sequence, 102; resources for, 92

students: and effective instruction, 10–11; role of, remixing, 12–13

Sutherland, L.M., 6

Swadener, B.B., 31

Swain, T., 14, 84

Symons, S., 56

T

Tanen, N., 42

teacher: and effective instruction, 9–10; role of, remixing, 12–13

technology, 1–2; and literacy, 79–80; remixing teacher/student roles and, 12–13

text(s): authentic, writing instruction and, 81–82; multiple, and critical thinking, 56–77; term, 18

text selection, and engagement, 6

texting/text messaging, 8f

think-aloud, 47, 86

Torgensen, J.K., 9

Tosh, P., 25

Townsend, D., 31

transmission models, of literacy instruction, 13

Truth, S., 88

Turner, K.H., 31

Turner, M.G., 28

Twitter, 8f

Tyack, D., 30

V

Van Zant, R., 23

Vasquez, V.M., 56

videos: digital, tools for, 44t; tools for, 44t; viral, 8f

vodcast, 8f

Vygotsky, L.S., 9, 18, 37

W

Wachtel, R., 23

Wardrop, J., 12

Web 2.0, 8f

Welles, O., 48

West, K., 18

Wigfield, A., 45

Wiki, 8f

Wikipedia, 8f, 17

will.i.am, 21, 23

Williams, N.G., 85t

Winkler, I., 35

Wise, R., 18

Wixson, K.K., 57

Wolfram, W., 30

writers' workshop, 79

writing: authentic text and, 81–82; Bubble Project, 71–75; critical consciousness and, 80–81; documentary poetry, 82–93; expanded definitions of, 79–80; expository, 93–97; literacy remix and, 78–99; research reports, 69; traditional instruction in, 78–79

Y

Yagelski, R.P., 11

YouTube, 8f

Z

Zevon, W., 23

Zhang, P., 15